A Guide to

PORT SUNLIGHT VILL.

A Guide to
PORT SUNLIGHT VILLAGE

including two tours of the village

Edward Hubbard and
Michael Shippobottom

LIVERPOOL UNIVERSITY PRESS

Published by
Liverpool University Press
4 Cambridge Street
Liverpool L69 7ZU

First published 1988
Reprinted, with corrections and amendments, 1990, 1996, 1998 and 2000
Second (revised) edition 2005
Third edition 2019

British Library Cataloguing-in-Publication data
A British Library CIP record is available

ISBN 978-1-786-94212-8

Typeset by Carnegie Book Production, Lancaster
Printed and bound by TJ International Ltd, Padstow, Cornwall, PL28 8RW

Contents

Preface to the 1988 Edition

This guide is based on the same writers' Architecture section of the catalogue which accompanied the exhibition *Lord Leverhulme*, presented at the Royal Academy by Unilever in 1980 to mark their Golden Jubilee. With the consent of Unilever plc, passages from the catalogue are here re-used. Reference may be made to the catalogue for details of sources, further Port Sunlight minutiae and consideration of Lord Leverhulme's architectural patronage as a whole, as well as for expert coverage of aspects of his collection. The present work has also drawn on *The Buildings of England: Cheshire*, by Nikolaus Pevsner and Edward Hubbard, 1971.

Mr Edward Morris of the National Museums & Galleries on Merseyside, at whose suggestion the guide was undertaken, has given assistance, encouragement and advice. At Port Sunlight help was received from Mr P. K. Hodson (Estates Manager), Mr M. C. Moore (Head of Information Services) and Miss Ailsa Bowers (Information Officer), all of UML Ltd. Thanks are due also to Miss Maureen Staniforth, Librarian and Information Officer at Unilever House.

Preface to the 2019 Edition

It is now forty years since Edward Hubbard generously involved me with him in contributing to the Royal Academy Exhibition on Lord Leverhulme, out of which emerged the first edition of this *Guide*. Looking back, I am sure 'Ted' would now wish, with me, to acknowledge the many others who contributed over a long period to our knowledge of Port Sunlight and Lord Leverhulme as an architectural patron: above all, our tutor at Manchester University, John Archer, for his much appreciated guidance and the many people still alive then who had known or worked for Lord Leverhulme and who kindly gave their time to meet. In particular, there were several meetings with James Lomax Simpson, Lever's favourite and most prolific architect, and a very lively eighty/ninety-year-old at the time, as well as meetings with: Ernest Prestwich, who as a student had designed the central area of the village; Sir Thomas Harley, solicitor to Lord Leverhulme; and, in Stornoway, Emily Macdonald, a niece of the first Lord Leverhulme. There were also several relatives of Lever architects. Particularly important were meetings with Halsall Owen, son of Geoffrey Owen, who at the time was still continuing the W. & S. Owen practice in Warrington; also 'Bunty' Elnyth Merryl Gurney, daughter of Segar Owen; and, in Lancaster, where the Mawson practice then also still continued under a grandson, Thomas P. Mawson. We must also acknowledge the help of the third Lord Leverhulme.

In connection with the present edition, thanks are due to the late Edward Morris, who initiated and continued strongly to support work on the *Guide*; Gavin Hunter, whose own writings provide additional information on the village; and, at Port Sunlight, Claire Tunstall of Unilever Archives; Paul Harris, Heather McGrath-Alcock, Katherine Lynch and formerly also Stuart Irwin, Lionel Bolland and Angharrad Hughes of the Port Sunlight Village Trust; Alyson Pollard and Sarah Lynch of National Museums Liverpool and formerly also Julian Treuherz; Ian Leith, Alyson Rogers and Neil Stephenson, formerly of English Heritage, National Monuments Record, now Historic England; William Meredith of Wirral archives, Caroline Furey of Bolton Archives; Mike Paddock; Rosemary Lomax-Simpson, Eitan Karol, Philip Cowan, Caroline Drake, Peter Howell, Peter Miller (USA), Caroline Lee, Joseph Sharples and our publishers Liverpool University Press, particularly Alison Welsby, and Rachel Chamberlain of Carnegie Book Production. As before, thanks are also due for permission to reproduce photographs to: Unilever Collections at Unilever Art, Archives and Records Management, Port Sunlight; Port Sunlight Museum; Bolton Library and Museum; British Architectural Library RIBA; Historic England and the Leverhulme family. Unless otherwise stated, other photographs are reproduced courtesy of National Museums, Liverpool. I am also most grateful to Colin Jackson and Mark Watson for additional photographs taken specially for the *Guide* and to Mark also for the cover image.

MHS 2019

Foreword

When I first joined the staff of the Walker Art Gallery in 1966, the largest room in the gallery was entirely devoted to an enormous model showing the future shape of Liverpool city centre. Few then doubted the wisdom of the City Planning Department, displayed in the colossal rectangular slabs of this vast and visionary model. Already, however, Edward Hubbard was meticulously cataloguing the historic buildings of Merseyside and beyond for Pevsner's *Buildings of England* volumes, and, under the auspices of the Victorian Society, the Liverpool Heritage Bureau, Diocesan Advisory Committees and other bodies, he was describing their beauties and defending their continued existence. His facts were always correct, his tone always measured and his grasp of planning law never doubted. His scholarship was, however, ultimately more influential than his advocacy, because the new concern for conservation of the last twenty-five years was primarily caused by public opinion, informed by a new generation of well-researched and intellectually stimulating architectural guide books. This is the last of those guide books to which he contributed. In it he and Michael Shippobottom describe, paradoxically, a comprehensive redevelopment scheme, engineered by an autocrat with powers unequalled even by a modern planning officer. But Edward Hubbard greatly admired William Hesketh Lever; it would be impossible to imagine two more different men, but both shared a humanity in their approach to architecture and a sensitivity in their appreciation of buildings which this book amply demonstrates – and which is the cause of the pride I feel in having commissioned it almost twenty years ago.

Edward Morris (1940–2016)
Late Curator of Fine Art at the Walker Art Gallery 2005

The Founder

William Hesketh Lever (1851–1925) was born in Bolton, the son of a successful wholesale grocer, and with a family background of Liberalism, Nonconformity and abstinence. At sixteen he entered the family firm, became a partner at twenty-one and soon expanded the already prosperous business beyond the confines of Bolton. In 1884 he began to specialise in one aspect of the grocery trade, namely the marketing of soap. Sold under the registered name 'Sunlight', it was initially made to his formula by various manufacturers, but the following year he founded the firm of Lever Brothers to make it independently. A factory was leased at Warrington, where production began in 1886. Despite this partnership with his brother James Darcy Lever (1854–1910), it is the powerful personality of W. H. Lever which dominates the story of Port Sunlight and the company.

Sunlight Soap differed from most current types in its superior ingredients, containing no silicate of soda and with more vegetable oil than tallow. Also – and this was a notable innovation – it was sold neatly packaged and stamped with its name. Business was boosted by efficient salesmanship and advertising, the scale of which expanded over the years, revealing Lever's seldom erring flair for astute publicity. With production having quickly risen from 20 to 450 tons of soap a week, new premises became necessary, and in 1888 construction of the works at Port Sunlight was begun. The enterprise steadily grew and so did Lever's personal wealth. From early on, expansion was international in scope; it was accompanied by the taking over of, and amalgamation with, other concerns, and a policy of gaining control over the supply of raw materials was pursued. Multiplicity of business (including the development of margarine manufacture) led, after the Great War, to the moving of headquarters from Port Sunlight to London, and in 1930 Lever Brothers and the Dutch Margarine Union merged to form the Unilever organisation.

The success of the early venture resulted in extension and alteration at the Warrington factory, the local architect William Owen being responsible. Owen received much subsequent employment from Lever and was involved in the creation of Port Sunlight, once it had become clear that the Warrington plant and its restricted site would have to be abandoned. Prompted by squalor seen in industrial Britain (Fig. 2) and by the social conscience which family background had engendered, Lever was determined from the first that a new factory would be accompanied by model housing for employees.

Fig. 1 Lever making a speech, in The Diamond at Port Sunlight, 1917, on the occasion of his elevation to the peerage. (Unilever Collections, Unilever Art, Archives and Records Management, Port Sunlight)

Fig. 2 Housing replaced at Port Sunlight. Dwellings as squalid as many an industrial slum occupied part of the village's marshland site. Duke of York Cottages, Brook Street and the foot of Primrose Hill now occupy this area. Photograph early or mid-1890s. (Unilever Collections, Unilever Art, Archives and Records Management, Port Sunlight)

Next to business, Lever's chief interest in life was architecture; he actively involved himself in the development of Port Sunlight village and worked in close collaboration with architects employed both there and elsewhere. Countless construction and planning schemes reflect his own visual tastes, as did the art collection which filled several of his own houses as well as the Lady Lever Art Gallery. Building was for him an end in itself and he spoke of his enthusiasm when addressing the Architectural Association in 1902. Between marriage in 1874 and his death he occupied thirteen houses in total, each of which he either built or to some extent either altered or enlarged. This passion was expressed in special doors and chimney-pieces introduced into the simple house in Bolton where he first lived after his marriage, no less than in successive rebuildings, remodellings and extensions at Thornton Manor on his rural Wirral estate.

Concern for architecture and planning motivated many of Lever's public benefactions, not least the gift to the nation of the great London palace of Stafford House, renamed Lancaster House at his wish. Instigated by Professor (Sir) Charles H. Reilly, he developed patronly interest in the Liverpool University School of Architecture, and of £91,000 libel damages awarded against the *Daily Mail* and other newspapers, c. 1907, some was devoted to saving from demolition Liverpool's eighteenth-century former Blue Coat School, and the remainder was donated to the university, in part to establish a Chair of Civic Design – a then pioneering venture. In Bolton he bought and restored the historic Hall-i'-th'-Wood, presenting it to the town as a museum; a sumptuous Congregational church was built at the expense of his brother and himself; he initiated the erection of new, unified premises for Bolton School and gave a public park to the town, though attempts to promote schemes of town planning and civic improvement came to nothing. At Rivington, not far away, he formed another public park and built a re-creation of the medieval Liverpool Castle beside one of Liverpool's Rivington Reservoirs. Rather than being a folly, this had serious didactic purpose, no less than had the opening of Rivington Hall as a museum and art gallery. Comparable in educational intent were 'period' rooms at the Lady Lever Art Gallery (Fig. 64) and the use of Hall-i'-th'-Wood as what amounted to an early instance of a folk museum.

'Altering the face of nature was with him a passion',[1] wrote Lever's son, and his imagination was stirred by the challenge of Port Sunlight's unpromising site. On the large agricultural estate which he amassed in Wirral, not only was the village of Thornton Hough embellished and largely rebuilt as a rural Port Sunlight, but some five miles of avenues were planted. With the landscape architect Thomas H. Mawson, Lever laid out spectacular gardens at Thornton Manor, at The Hill (his London home at Hampstead) and at Rivington. On the bleak moorland hillside of Rivington Pike, at the edge of the Pennines and high above the reser-

Fig. 3 Lever seen holding the reins, with a party in front of Bridge Cottage, Port Sunlight c. 1900. His wife, wearing a floral hat, is sitting on the far right. Lever and his wife lived intermittently at Bridge Cottage for periods around 1893–97. The photograph was taken by Edward John Jenkins, a manager at the factory and village resident. (Port Sunlight Museum)

voirs and the park, was built The Bungalow (or Roynton Cottage), commanding stupendous views and set amidst acres of lawns, terraces, loggias and lakes, all formed on the precipitous and inhospitable slopes. The first house there was burnt by a suffragette and its successor demolished by Liverpool Corporation.

Lever's interests and tastes must have received guidance and impetus from the social contact that he maintained with architects, particularly Jonathan Simpson, a life-long friend. Stylistically, Lever's outlook was that of the late phase of historicism and, uncommitted to any theory or philosophy of architecture, his taste was eclectic. Generally he favoured classical interiors, but was disposed towards the 'Old English' of vernacular and Elizabethan revivalism and greatly admired the timber-framing of north-west England. Quality of materials and craftsmanship and perfection of detail are hallmarks of Lever's building, and are no less characteristic of him than are the boldness and breadth of vision which inspired Port Sunlight and the great gardens. Though he favoured grand formal planning, Lever's taste in classical architecture was for academic refinement rather than heavy Baroque.

The company's concerns overseas engaged his attention and he took direct interest in the design of factories, and in the planning of model settlements for native workers on Lever Brothers' plantations in the Belgian Congo.

Lever was created a baronet in 1911 and a baron in 1917, when he took the maiden name of his late wife, Elizabeth Hulme, to form the title Leverhulme. She had been a childhood friend, and was apparently a person of simple tastes and easy-going nature – the perfect foil for her ambitious, energetic husband. She died in 1913, having been Lady

Lever, but never Lady Leverhulme. Hence the name of the art gallery which is her memorial. In 1922 Lord Leverhulme was raised in the peerage to the rank of viscount.

Dictatorial and vain, but astonishingly generous, Lever was a man of contradiction and paradox. Ruthless tycoon and autocrat, patron and philanthropist, the magnificence of his residences belied ascetic personal habits: he slept in partly open-air bedrooms which were created at several of his houses. He enjoyed a placid family life and a flamboyant public and commercial career generously punctuated with drama and incident – business warfare, the *Daily Mail* libel action and other litigation, the burning of Roynton Cottage, his mutilation of an Augustus John portrait and, at the end of his life, costly and abortive schemes for improvement and development of the Outer Hebridean isles of Lewis and Harris.

While at Port Sunlight there were criticisms of too much control exercised over the lives of its inhabitants: G. K. Chesterton settled out of court after Lever threatened to sue him for accusing Lever Brothers of 'slavery in Port Sunlight' and, in connection with the former Belgian Congo, there have been more recent claims of flouting of native rights and freedoms.[2]

Lever was a man of his time and needs to be judged by the standards of his day, and after the death of his wife, with increasing loneliness and deafness, as well as some loss of control of the company, some of his earlier business and personal skills may have become blunted. Undoubtedly a complex and many-sided visionary, he remained a Congregationalist, a Gladstonian Liberal (representing Wirral in parliament 1906–1909) and, above all, a fervent disciple of Smilesian self-help. Attesting to wide reading and careful thought, his business philosophies and ideas on housing, planning and related social issues were expounded in numerous lectures and published addresses, as well as in less formal speeches.

Though Lever maintained that he always acted only for sound business reasons, the happiness and well-being of the ordinary man were genuinely close to his heart. In an avowed spirit of enlightened self-interest, Lever sought to improve working conditions in industry, displaying humanitarianism, albeit with what would today be an impossible degree of paternalism. He introduced shorter working hours and benefit and welfare schemes and provisions, and in 1909 the plan of employees' co-partnership in Lever Brothers was established. Direct profit sharing was eschewed, and the creation of Port Sunlight and its communal facilities was the prime instance of what, in seeking a healthy and contented workforce, Lever termed 'prosperity sharing'.

Notes
1 Viscount Leverhulme, *Viscount Leverhulme by his Son*, 1927, p. 85.
2 See Brian Lewis, *So Clean: Lord Leverhulme, Soap and Civilization*, 2008, pp. 154–98.

Background

Both the location and the timing of Lever's birth are significant: Bolton le Moors, to give the town its full ancient name, was a fast-growing manufacturing centre with industries of cotton spinning, engineering and mining. A canal from Manchester had opened in 1797, while Robert Stephenson's Bolton and Leigh Railway opened in 1828, pre-dating the more famous Liverpool and Manchester Railway by two years. But Bolton has a medieval background: it received its Market Charter in 1251 and it was the only town in the English Civil War to suffer a major civilian massacre. The town was strongly Parliamentarian and its nonconformist, radical traits caused it to be given the moniker of 'the Geneva of the North'. It was in the Bolton area where the American Shaker movement began – but then the waves of emigration in the nineteenth century led to many American connections besides those established through cotton. Two of America's leading artists, Thomas Cole (1801–48) and Thomas Moran (1837–1926), for example, were both born in Bolton.

In the early nineteenth century, industrial progress was accompanied by economic fluctuations and political and social unrest: a Luddite riot resulted in the destruction of a local mill (following which three men and a boy were hanged) and there was a Chartist riot in the town in 1839 followed by the so-called 'Plug Riots' in 1842. Manchester's Peterloo Massacre was not yet a dim memory at the time of Lever's birth, and because of the major trade recession in the late 1830s and early 1840s, Bolton was said to be the most distressed town in Britain, with no rates levied at all in 1840–41. However, various civic improvements were begun with, for example, street gas lighting from 1819; fresh water supply from moorland reservoirs from 1822; a library and newsroom in 1825; Mechanics Institute in 1826 and then, after Lever's birth, a Market Hall in 1853; a new town hall in 1866–73 and replacement parish church, 1868–71. Lever's later youth was passed in the shadow of the Lancashire cotton famine, a period of further distress and poverty caused by the stoppage of imports of American cotton during the American Civil War. This unsettled local background, alleviated by prominent public works and private philanthropy, shaped Lever's beliefs in the need to improve radically workers' security, welfare and, above all, housing.

At Port Sunlight two separate traditions in the history of town planning met for the first time. On the one hand there was the picturesque visual tradition derived from eighteenth-century landscape design as translated into the semi-urban terms of Nash's Regent's Park and the Regency suburbs, spas and watering places, with their villas and terraces in silvan settings. This tradition, with townscape subservient to landscape, flourished in Victorian times. It guided the planning of resorts such as Bournemouth and Torquay, and inspired countless well-to-do suburbs, with curving tree-lined roads, in London and the expanding industrial towns and cities. The ideal was continued in the influential Bedford Park, at Turnham Green, begun in 1875 as a self-consciously 'aesthetic' middle-class 'garden suburb', from 1877 with work by Norman Shaw.

The other tradition – a social one – was that of materially decent conditions for the urban working classes. The movement for housing and sanitary reform, dating from the 1840s, included Sir Edwin Chadwick, Lord Shaftesbury, Samuel Peabody and Octavia Hill among its campaigners, and the 1851 Housing and 1875 Health Acts among its achievements. The special movement for the provision by individual industrialists of housing and social amenities in connection with their factories may be traced back to such schemes as Richard Arkwright's village at Cromford, Derbyshire (from 1771); Samuel Greg's Styal, Cheshire (from 1784); David Dale's New Lanark (founded 1783 but developed and made famous by Robert Owen from 1800); and the Union Ironworks' Butetown in the Rhymney Valley, Glamorgan (from 1802). More impersonal were the several towns established by Victorian railway companies, but significant among model industrial communities built, with social facilities and to orderly plans, by well-motivated employers were Edwin Ackroyd's Copley (c. 1847–53) and his Ackroyden (by (Sir) Gilbert Scott and W. H. Crossland, from 1859), both near Halifax. The most important and extensive example is Sir Titus Salt's town of Saltaire, near Shipley (by Lockwood & Mawson, from c. 1850). Among many lesser known instances are (all near Bolton) the Ashworths' New Eagley Village and Egerton, and (from c. 1840) Robert Gardner's settlement at Barrow Bridge. Also, and within a mile of Port Sunlight, there is the Bromborough Pool Village of Price's Patent Candle Co. (by Julian Hill, from 1853).

In their housing and their layouts these places did not depart from the utilitarian rows of urban terraces and grid plans. They merely improved on them, and open spaces were generally little more than adjuncts. It is true that architectural aspiration and picturesque siting may characterise rural model cottages, and that the achievements of Victorian improving country landowners working in a tradition with its roots in the eighteenth century have tended to be under-estimated in assessments of housing reform. Yet little direct comparison can be made between estate villages in an agricultural community and the problems of the towns. The historical significance of Port Sunlight lies in its

Fig. 4 Model Housing in Halstead Street, the Haulgh, Bolton, designed by Jonathan Simpson for the Chadwick Trustees and erected 1883–84 – i.e. just four years before work on Port Sunlight started. The houses survive and have been modernised, involving changes to the external joinery and the removal of the chimney stacks. (Copyright Bolton Council. From the collection of Bolton Library and Museum)

unprecedented combination of model industrial housing, and on a considerable scale at that, with the tradition of the silvan suburb, in which greenery and picturesque effect form integral elements in spacious planning.

It is not known to what extent Lever may have been familiar with Saltaire and other precursors, though in his youth he must have known Barrow Bridge, which, having been visited by the Prince Consort and Disraeli, enjoyed local fame, and undoubtedly he was aware of public-spirited Bolton industrialists and their benefactions. Moreover, his friend Jonathan Simpson designed some terraces of model cottages, built 1884–86 in the Haulgh, Bolton, for a trust established by Dr Samuel Chadwick, a noted local worthy (Fig. 4). Remarks of the philanthropic industrialist Joseph Strutt of Belper, quoted by Samuel Smiles, anticipate Lever's concept of 'prosperity sharing' and must have touched a receptive chord within him: 'it would be ungrateful in me not to employ a portion of the fortune I possess in promoting the welfare of those amongst whom I live, and by whose industry I have been aided in its organisation'.[1]

When travelling, both on business and otherwise, Lever was a keen observer of architecture. On an early visit to Chatsworth he may well have seen the village of Edensor (rebuilt by (Sir) Joseph Paxton and John Robertson, 1838–42, for the sixth Duke of Devonshire) and he must have been aware of the massive programme of improvements carried out by the Chester architect John Douglas (whose firm he employed at Port Sunlight) on the first Duke of Westminster's Eaton Estate. He appreciated the beauties of English country towns and villages, and in 1887, just prior to the founding of Port Sunlight, a holiday in the West Country included visits to Dorchester, Blandford, Shaftesbury and Salisbury. It is believed that in the course of continental travel he saw Agneta Park, the model village of the Dutch industrialist van Marken at Delft, but at a time when Port Sunlight was already well advanced. Planned in the English manner of Nash, London and Paxton, with buildings integrated in parkland, Agneta Park was begun just before Port Sunlight, and each village subsequently featured in the other's literature.

Lever was no doubt also kept well-informed of current architectural and planning developments by the architects with whom he was on terms of close friendship, particularly the Simpson and Owen families and then later Thomas Mawson and Professor Charles Reilly of Liverpool University. Lever was a reader of both Ruskin[2] and William Morris, and his library included several notable architectural works. Walter Creese, writing in *The Search for Environment*,[3] questioned whether Lever might also have been influenced by the idealised medieval street temporarily erected at the Royal Jubilee Exhibition in Manchester of 1887. Given that Lever Brothers exhibited a model of the Warrington factory at the exhibition it must be assumed that Lever attended, and some influence of this 'Old Manchester and Salford', recreated at a stroke, must be acknowledged, not least its free-flowing plan and varied jettied and gabled frontages. Moreover, there was also a Hulme Hall and a Poets' Corner, again anticipating later features of Port Sunlight (Fig. 5).

Accounts of Lever's more distant journeys were published in the Lever Brothers' house journal *Progress*, and that of his first voyage round the world in 1892 appeared in book form as *Following the Flag*. Here he recorded impressions of towns and cities, noting favourably such features as spacious boulevards or provision of parks, and, most important of all, his reaction to the then unfinished Columbian Exposition (World's Fair), in Chicago: 'For picturesqueness of situation, beauty and extent of buildings, arrangement, conception and general execution it leaves nothing to be desired … In addition to size which itself is always impressive, each building from a purely architectural point-of-view is well-conceived, duly proportioned and most admirably executed.'[4] The exhibition (at which Lever Brothers were represented by a lavish stand) (see page 76), held in 1893, initiated the 'City Beautiful' movement in America, giving as it did impetus and inspiration to revival of classical architecture and concepts of civic design. These left their mark on later developments at Port Sunlight as much as on Lever himself, no doubt reinforcing his belief in the virtues of good planning, with defined order to the townscape.

Housing erected in connection with the locomotive works of the Lancashire & Yorkshire Railway at Horwich, near Bolton (c. 1886) was criticised by Lever. He noted the opportunity wasted by building 'on the same crowded plan' as had prevailed around the company's old works in Manchester.[5] He expounded his views on living conditions in an address of 1898, in which he referred to the work of Lord Shaftesbury, and to having studied Charles Booth's *Life and Labour of the People of London*. Lever said, 'A child that knows nothing of God's earth, of green fields, or sparkling brooks, of breezy hill and springy heather, and whose mind is stored with none of the beauties of nature, but knows only the

Market Sted Lane.

Fig. 5 Old Manchester and Salford. The recreation of old buildings and streets from Manchester and Salford city centres formed a key attraction at the Royal Jubilee Exhibition in Manchester in 1887 and was designed by the Manchester architect Alfred Darbyshire. This must have been a powerful influence on Lever both in terms of the attractive recreation of an idealised medieval street scene but also in terms of its educational interest in connection with his later museum involvements. The main contractor was Robert Neill and Sons who were to be responsible shortly afterwards for the factory at Port Sunlight. (Alfred Darbyshire, *The Book of Olde Manchester and Salford*, Royal Jubilee Exhibition, 1887)

drunkenness prevalent in the hideous slum it is forced to live in, and whose walks abroad have never extended beyond the corner public-house and the pawnshop, cannot be benefited by education. Such children grow up depraved, and become a danger and terror to the State; wealth-destroyers instead of wealth-producers.'[6] Overcrowded layouts were condemned: 'there can be no reason why man should not make towns livable and healthy ... just as much subject to the beneficent influence of bright sunshine, fresh air, flowers, and plants, as the country'.[7] As for flats, 'All tenement dwellings,' he said in 1907, 'flats, and such devices for crowding a maximum amount of humanity in a minimum amount of ground space are destructive of healthy life'.[8] He went on: 'I am positive, from all the statistics available, that the most healthy conditions of the human race are obtained where the home unit exists in a self-contained house, with the living rooms on the ground floor and the bedrooms on the floor immediately over'.[9]

'The picture of a cottage crowned with a thatched roof, and with clinging ivy and climbing roses and a small garden foreground suggesting old-fashioned perfume of flowers and a home in which dwell content and happiness, appeals straight to the heart of each of us, and there are few who can resist its quiet, peaceful influence for good.'[10] Though the word 'picture' is here to be taken literally, meaning a painting of the scene described, Lever's approval of a *beau ideal* cottage home is clear, together with his belief that 'Art and the Beautiful unconsciously create an atmosphere in which happiness and the virtues grow and flourish'.[11]

In seeking a site for the new soap factory begun in 1888, space for a residential village had been a prime consideration; Port Sunlight tenancy was, from the first, confined to company employees and pensioners and, in accordance with the theory of prosperity sharing, no realistic return on the cost of outlay was intended. In his speech at the banquet which followed the ceremony of cutting the first sod, Lever remarked, 'it is my hope, and my brother's hope … to build houses in which our work-people will be able to live and be comfortable. Semi-detached houses, with gardens back and front, in which they will be able to know more about the science of life than they can in a back slum, and in which they will learn that there is more enjoyment in life than in the mere going to and returning from work, and looking forward to Saturday night to draw their wages.'[12]

Notes

1 Samuel Smiles, *Self Help*, 1895 edition, p. 216 (first edition published 1859).
2 See, for example, his reference to *The Seven Lamps of Architecture* in a speech given to the RIBA following the Annual Dinner in 1909. RIBA Journal, vol. 16 (12 June 1909). Works by both Ruskin and Morris featured in the catalogue of Lever's library in the sale catalogue of 1925.
3 Walter Creese, *The Search for Environment*, 1966, p. 128.
4 W. H. Lever, *Following the Flag*, 1893, p. 7.
5 *The Builder*, vol. 82, 1902, p. 318. The reference was made in discussion following the delivery of his paper on *The Buildings Erected at Port Sunlight and Thornton Hough* to the Architectural Association.
6 W. H. Lever, *Land for Houses*, paper read before North End Liberal Club (Birkenhead), Tuesday 4 October 1898, p. 5.
7 *Ibid.*, p. 2.
8 *Visit of International Housing Conference to Port Sunlight*, 9 August 1907, Chairman's Address, pp. 8–9.
9 *Ibid.*, p. 9.
10 W. H. Lever, *Art and Beauty and the City*, three addresses, 1915, p. 6.
11 *Ibid.*, p. 6.
12 *Messrs. Lever's New Soap Works, Port Sunlight, Cheshire. Full Reports of the Ceremony of Cutting the First Sod, and Proceedings at the Inaugural Banquet*, 1888, pp. 28–29.

3

Planning and Development

Port Sunlight, named after the product that had so rapidly outgrown the Warrington works, was inaugurated on 3 March 1888, when Mrs W. H. Lever performed the ceremony of cutting the first sod. The site, in Wirral, had been chosen by Lever and William Owen after extensive searching. It allowed room for future expansion, was near a potential source of labour, and had facilities for road, rail and water transport. Bromborough Pool, an inlet of the River Mersey, provided a dock for the factory. There was also the advantage of cheapness, for much of the land was of poor quality – the site over which the village ultimately extended was marshy, and traversed by tidal inlets from the Pool in the form of muddy creeks. These followed roughly an E-plan, with a main channel (running north–south parallel with the river) and three western branches. The few buildings on the site included some insanitary housing near the north-west corner (Fig. 2).

Initially, some 24 acres were purchased for the factory followed by 32 acres for the village.[1] The factory, soon to be expanded, was completed in 1889, and in 1889–90 an entrance lodge and several blocks of cottages were built. The cottages at the junction of what were to become Bolton and Greendale Roads comprised 28 dwellings, and, like the factory itself, were designed by Owen (Figs 6–8). A set of larger houses followed in 1890, and in 1891–92 came a further group of cottages, a shop (later Post Office) and the village's first place of assembly in the form of Gladstone Hall. Some or all of these buildings of 1891–92 were designed in limited competition, with those taking part including Owen, the Liverpool firm of Grayson & Ould, and probably Douglas & Fordham of Chester.

Further cottages, shops and public buildings were added in 1893–97, thus completing the original village, which occupies the south-west corner of the later expanded community. The layout was apparently designed by Owen, on the basis of a plan by Lever. It is outward-looking, with sets of cottages facing a railway and the factory. Then, turning in on itself, it encloses the former continuation of the south branch channel, landscaped and spanned by a footbridge and known as The Dell (Figs 9, 10). Though this early portion remains the most attractive and visually satisfying area of the village, the problems posed by the topography were not fully solved. The curves of The Dell, and the adaptation of straight building lines to follow them, conflict with a basically rectangular concept of street plan. For the most part, the sets of cottages

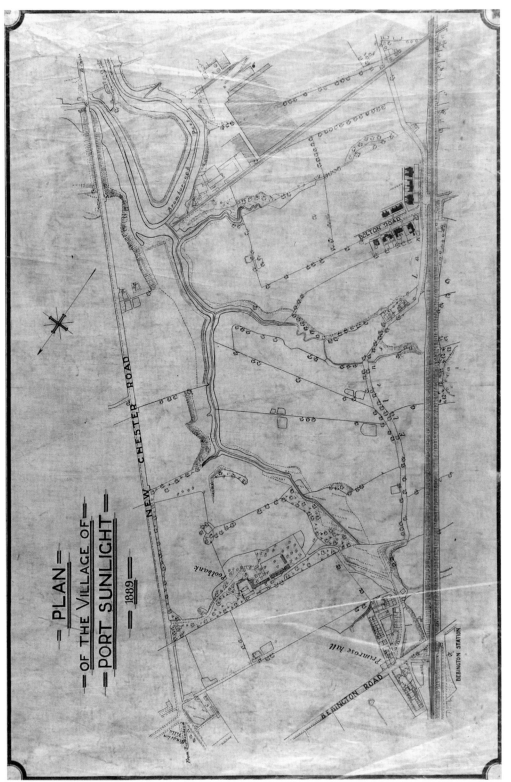

Fig. 6 Plan of the village, 1889. All that has so far been built is part of the first group of cottages (William Owen, 1889–90) at what was to become the junction of Bolton and Greendale Roads. The rest of the site is mostly marsh, traversed by tidal inlets running from Bromborough Pool in the SE (top RH) corner; the slum housing is at 'Primrose Hill' near the NW corner. (Unilever Collections, Unilever Art, Archives and Records Management, Port Sunlight)

Fig. 7 Nos. 14–18 Bolton Road (Owen, 1889). The first cottages erected at Port Sunlight; destroyed in Second World War; commemorative plaque recorded a reproduction having been awarded a Grand Prix at the 1910 Brussels Exhibition. (Unilever Collections, Unilever Art, Archives and Records Management, Port Sunlight)

Fig. 8 A view of Bolton Road in its incomplete state c. 1891 showing the road terminating in the near distance. On the left, the present No. 1 Bolton Road was at that time two houses, Nos. 1 and 3; the architect J. J. Talbot lived in No. 3 during the late 1890s. On the right-hand side the distant block is that recorded as being the first to be erected in the village, Nos. 14–18 Bolton Road. (*Souvenir of Port Sunlight*, 1891, Unilever)

enclose small and awkwardly shaped spaces at the rear (Fig. 11), though one of these areas was large enough to serve as allotment gardens.

When work commenced, the extent to which the village might grow was not foreseen, and during a voyage round the world in 1892, Lever, according to his own statement, made a plan for future expansion. It seems that it was along the lines of this plan that development proceeded. In 1892 the land required for the scheme was not all owned by the company, and was acquired gradually, until the village reached its present size of c. 130 acres.

The dominating boundary lines are straight, comprising the factory and Wood Street on the south (this alignment having been dictated by a quarry tramway whose lines remained until c. 1912, Fig. 13), the railway on the west, and Bebington and New Chester Roads on the north and east respectively. The extended plan continued the precedent of an outward-looking perimeter, with housing facing the two outer roads (Fig. 14), and the buildings already erected opposite the railway being continued as the enfilade of Greendale Road. With an especially pleasing series of cottages, this presents a deliberately impressive public face to the railway, which in pre-Beeching days carried main-line passenger trains. Within, the layout was dictated by the channels, which penetrated into the heart of the site, and rendered the areas available for building awkward in size or shape or both. Again with a precedent in the earlier portion of the village, a system of superblocks (to use a later town planning term) was adopted, each with many blocks of cottages around its perimeter, and

Fig. 9 Lyceum (Douglas & Fordham, 1894–96) with Dell Bridge (Douglas & Fordham, 1894). (Colin Jackson)

Fig. 10 The Dell and buildings of 1892 on N side of Park Road. Shows, L to R: Part of Nos. 1–7 (Owen); Nos. 9–17 (Owen); part of Nos. 19–23 (Douglas & Fordham). Photograph 1966. (Historic England Archives)

Fig. 11 An early superblock interior. Behind S side of Park Road (1893 and 1895) looking E to rear of Poets' Corner (1894). One similar early enclosure, and nearly all later ones, were large enough to contain allotments. Photograph mid-1890s. (Unilever Collections, Unilever Art, Archives and Records Management, Port Sunlight)

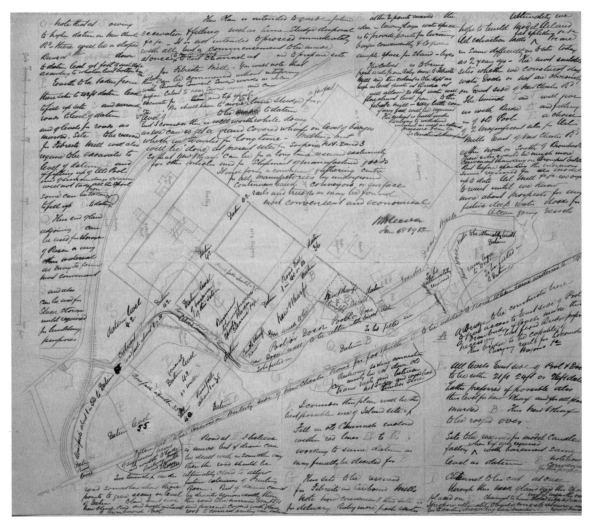

Fig. 12 Sketch plan drawn by Lever for the future expansion of the Port Sunlight factory, dated 18 January 1912. New Chester Road is shown running diagonally up from the bottom left-hand corner, with north to the right. The circuitous course of the Bromborough Pool channel, giving waterborne access to the factory, is shown here redirected to give a direct approach to the works – and, regarding which, Lever's notes instruct that work is to begin immediately. This is a typical example of the very detailed instructions Lever would lay down for his architects and surveyors, in sketch plan form, to indicate what he had in mind. (Unilever Collections, Unilever Art, Archives and Records Management, Port Sunlight)

enclosing allotment gardens and areas where washing would be hidden from public gaze. Incorporation of allotments at the centre of each super-block became a key feature of the village: an expression of Lever's belief in providing improved living conditions, a healthy alternative to the social evils of the time – drink and gambling – and moral lessons to be gained from successful cultivation. Special areas were reserved for children's allotments. As Lever said: 'a child with a garden soon learns that if that garden is neglected, it becomes full of weeds'. Produce was awarded prizes

Fig. 13 Wood Street, seen in 1897, with the rails of the earlier quarry tramway still intact, one of the determinants of the plan of the village. The factory and offices' East Wing are visible to the right. This is one of a number of photographs taken by the celebrated architectural photographer Bedford Lemere. (Historic England Archives)

Fig. 14 Nos 268–274 New Chester Road (Douglas & Fordham), showing the original rural setting and outward-looking boundaries of the village. (Unilever Collections, Unilever Art, Archives and Records Management, Port Sunlight)

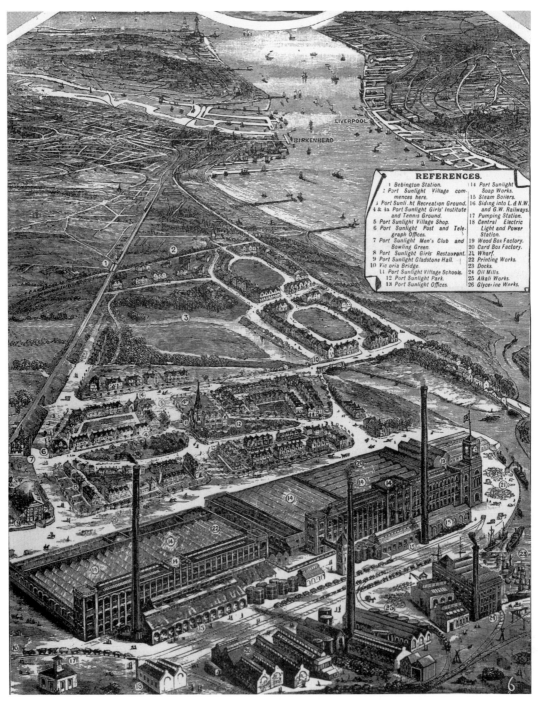

REFERENCES.

1 Bebington Station.
2 Port Sunlight Village commences here.
3 Port Sunlight Recreation Ground.
4 & 4a Port Sunlight Girls' Institute and Tennis Ground.
5 Port Sunlight Village Shop.
6 Port Sunlight Post and Telegraph Offices.
7 Port Sunlight Men's Club and Bowling Green.
8 Port Sunlight Girls Restaurant.
9 Port Sunlight Gladstone Hall.
10 Victoria Bridge.
11 Port Sunlight Village Schools.
12 Port Sunlight Park.
13 Port Sunlight Offices.
14 Port Sunlight Soap Works.
15 Steam Boilers.
16 Siding into L.&N.W. and G.W. Railways.
17 Pumping Station.
18 Central Electric Light and Power Station.
19 Wood Box Factory.
20 Card Box Factory.
21 Wharf.
22 Printing Works.
23 Docks.
24 Oil Mills.
25 Alkali Works.
26 Glycerine Works.

Fig. 15 Bird's-eye view, 1898. In the foreground is the factory: to right, No. 1 Soapery (1888–89, Owen) with its corner belvedere tower and its wharf on Bromborough Pool; to left, extensions to No. 1 Soapery (1893) and No. 2 Soapery with offices (1895–96, Owen), here shown at maximum later extent and not as existing in 1898. Behind it can be seen the first stage of the village, built 1889–97 around The Dell. Beyond, the incomplete state is apparent, with the perimeter partly built up and the centre still largely open and crossed by tidal creeks. (*Illustrated London News*, vol. 113, 1898, p. 563, Fig. 6)

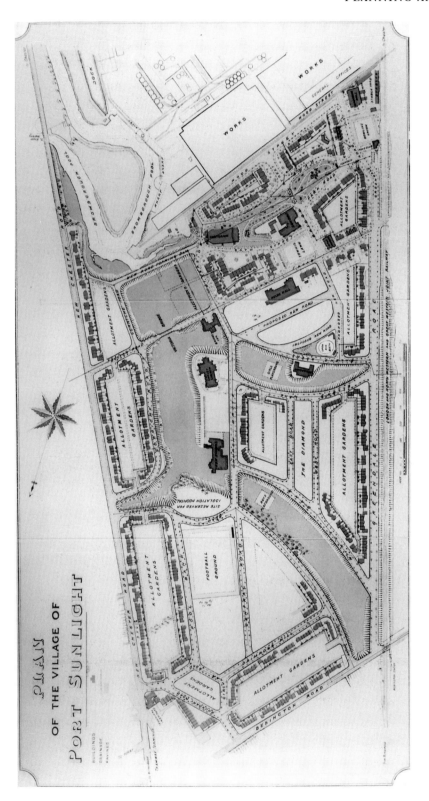

Fig. 16 Plan of the village, 1905. The earliest portion, 1889–97, encloses The Dell (the former S branch channel) at the SW (bottom RH) corner. In contrast, most of the rest of the layout is on the enlarged superblock pattern, with sets of cottages enclosing allotments. Most of the outward-looking perimeter has now been completed; some building has also taken place in the centre, planned around the channels. The position of the main inlet (with Church Drive Schools,

Christ Church and the Bridge Inn along its W bank) is discernible, as are the N and middle branches. However, a dam cutting the channels off from Bromborough Pool, near the SE corner, had by this time permitted some of them to be partly filled in. (W. H. Lever, *The Buildings Erected at Port Sunlight and Thornton Hough*, 2nd edn, 1905)

Fig. 17 Children's Allotments. The view is looking north from behind the Hulme Hall, around 1905, with the timber-boarded gymnasium shown in its original position before relocation to suit the Prestwich plan for the centre of the village. (Children's Allotments 1905 PS.61.1, Unilever Art, Archives and Records Management, Port Sunlight)

at an annual horticultural show, to which Lever invited guests, such as his friends the landscape architect and planner Thomas Mawson and the sculptors William Goscombe John and Derwent Wood. In this, the village provides a key example of the success of the national allotment movement – highlighted by the series of Allotment Acts at the turn of the century which aimed at encouraging their provision and regularising their use. Speaking in 1902, Lever regarded allotments as 'the very safety valve of the village',[2] and after the First World War, at a time of concerns about the spread of Bolshevism, even noted that, because of gardening, he didn't think 'we breed many Bolsheviks in Port Sunlight',[3] a subject (though without specific reference to allotments) raised by one Russian visitor, who noted to Margaret Stansgate, mother of the politician Tony Benn, that if Russia had had a Port Sunlight the Revolution would never have happened.[4]

The very size of the superblocks minimised the irregularities of plan resulting from the curving roads skirting the edges of the branch channels. Among the routes of communication is Bolton Road, aligned on the medieval spire of Bebington church and following the line of a former field boundary. (Other street names similarly have associations with Lever's native town.) It was carried across the main channel by the Victoria Bridge, the erection of which in 1897 opened up for development the eastern portion of the site, which Lever acquired in 1895–96.

Intensive activity took place from 1898, and by the turn of the century well over 400 houses were in existence, with the perimeter almost entirely built up, and a start having been made in the centre (Fig. 15).

With legal rights having been obtained over them, the channels were culverted (marked by conspicuous vent pipes), filled in to above high-water mark, and cut off from Bromborough Pool by a dam in 1901–1902 (Figs 18–20). It was intended that, like The Dell, they would remain as permanent landscape features, serving as parks and recreation grounds. They were, however, completely filled in and levelled, mostly in 1909–10, and in 1910 a competition for a revised plan for the completion of the village was held among students of the Liverpool School of Architecture and the Department of Civic Design. The winner was Ernest Prestwich, a third-year student at the School of Architecture.

The central feature of the plan hitherto had been The Diamond, a space with two parallel sides cut off at either end by sweeping roads skirting the branch channels – to the north Windy Bank and to the south The Causeway, then called Ellen's Lane. Except for Windy Bank (which, with Lower Road further north, remains the best illustration of housing following the line of a now-vanished channel) little of this layout had been built up by 1910, though the church (1902–1904) had been sited at the east end of The Causeway (Fig. 16). Prestwich's plan involved

Fig. 18 Looking W across the main channel, still tidal, with the Victoria Bridge (Owen, 1897) and Bridge Inn (Grayson & Ould, 1900). Immediately L of the inn are the gables of Nos. 1–8 Riverside (Grayson & Ould, 1896) and to the R, in distance, Hulme Hall (W. & S. Owen, 1900–1901). One of the factory's tall chimneys is also visible. Photograph c. 1901. (Unilever Collections, Unilever Art, Archives and Records Management, Port Sunlight)

the extension of The Diamond into a major formal element, the conversion of The Causeway into a second broad vista at right angles to it, aligned on the church, and the formation of roads radiating eastwards from the church. A formal square of public buildings, including an art gallery, was planned south of The Causeway, linking the church with existing buildings (Hulme Hall and the Bridge Inn) in Bolton Road (Figs 21, 22). The plan was, in its broad aspects, carried out, with revisions made by Lever and James Lomax Simpson (son of Lever's friend Jonathan Simpson) and with Mawson also involved. The site of the art gallery was transferred to the north end of The Diamond, making the axis an even more dominant element in the village than Prestwich had intended, and with the other public buildings omitted, Bolton Road remained unsatisfactorily related to the formal layout. In 1910, a timber gymnasium, first built in 1902, was moved from its site in The Causeway and re-erected next to the swimming baths (also of 1902), for the retention of which Prestwich had allowed. Both have since been demolished. The roads radiating from the church were laid out, and Lomax Simpson designed cottages for them, but these were never built (Figs 21, 22).

Thus a classically conceived *beaux arts* plan was imposed upon the partially completed village, the commencement of which had been on very different lines – the lines of an informal and picturesque response to features of the terrain now obliterated. Except for The Dell, which still remains, the last section of channel to survive seems to have been in the angle between Bolton Road and Water Street. It served as children's allotments, and was apparently levelled in 1914, and The Ginnel built on part of the site.

Addressing the International Housing Conference on its visit to Port Sunlight in 1907, Lever maintained that '[the] building of ten to twelve houses to the acre is the maximum that ought to be allowed … Houses should be built a minimum of 15 feet from the roadway … every house should have space available in the rear for vegetable garden. Open spaces for recreation should be laid out at frequent and convenient centres … A home requires a greensward and garden in front of it, just as much as a cup requires a saucer.'[5]. Maintenance of the Port Sunlight saucers, initially entrusted to tenants, was soon taken over by the company, to ensure uniform neatness. The present free and open character dates from the 1920s, when garden railings were removed. With gardens, broad tree-lined roads, communal open spaces (mostly on the sites of the channels) as well as the superblock enclosures, the overall density is well below the intended maximum of ten houses per acre.

As Gavin Hunter has shown, across New Chester Road housing on the Woodhead Estate was initially conceived as an extension to the village, its development given impetus by the pressures for additional local housing generated by the demands of the factory in the First World War.[6] (Port Sunlight's contribution to the war effort, in addition to its

Fig. 19 Christ Church (W. & S. Owen, 1902–1904) has joined the group beside the channel, now drained. Photograph c. 1905. (Unilever Collections, Unilever Art, Archives and Records Management, Port Sunlight)

Fig. 20 From similar viewpoint as Fig. 15, showing the channel partly filled in. Visible between the Bridge Inn and Christ Church is the gymnasium (W. & S. Owen, 1902) on its original site in the middle of The Causeway (cf. Fig. 20). This is one of a number of photographs taken by the local photographer, J. G. Davies, who lived in the village and worked in the Lever Brothers Printing Department. Photograph c. 1907. (Unilever Collections, Unilever Art, Archives and Records Management, Port Sunlight)

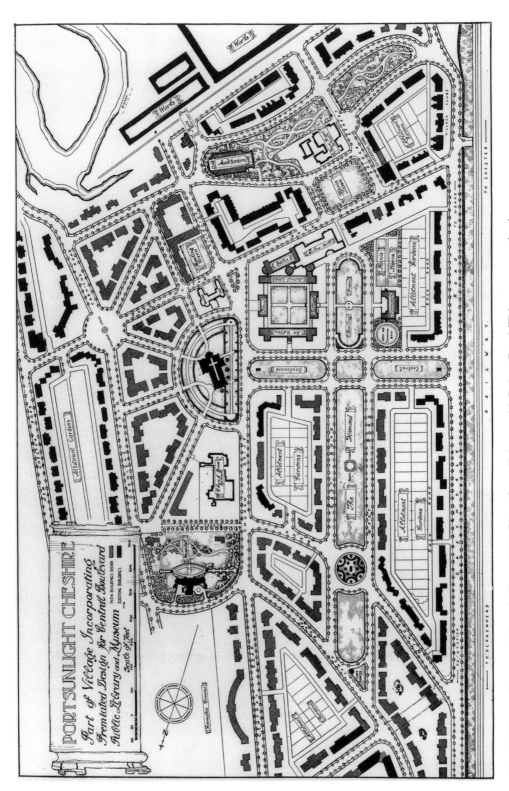

Fig. 21 Scheme for completion of village, 1910. Plan of the winning entry, by Ernest Prestwich, in the competition held after the channels had nearly all been filled in. Strong formality is introduced, with The Diamond and The Causeway as major intersecting axes; a square of public buildings (including an art gallery) links up with Bolton Road. This group remained unexecuted, as did housing shown on the site of the main channel, E of the church. At the N end of The Diamond (where the art gallery was in fact built) a clock tower was intended. (Thomas H. Mawson, *Civic Art*, 1911, p. 283, Fig. 239)

Fig. 22 Scheme for completion of the village, 1910. Perspective by Robert Atkinson illustrating the proposals as developed by T. H. Mawson, looking towards Christ Church from the railway. Atkinson was a brilliant perspectivist and seen here at his most beguiling with this impression of boulevards of almost Parisian splendour laid out in the heart of the village. (Thomas H. Mawson, *Civic Art*, 1911, p. 278, Fig. 235)

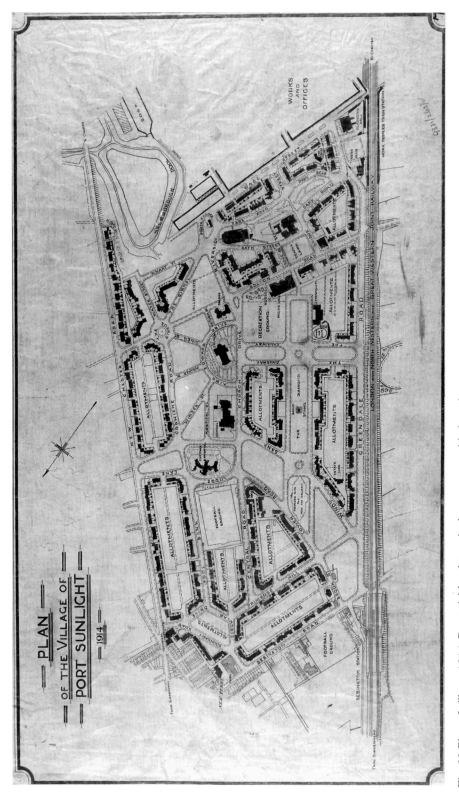

Fig. 23 Plan of village, 1914. Prestwich's scheme is shown executed in broad outline, but revised and modified. The public buildings are omitted and a site at the N end of The Diamond is reserved for the art gallery. Cottages have been built flanking The Diamond, though the roads radiating from the church are not built up. The earlier gymnasium has been moved and re-erected next to the swimming bath at the SE corner of the intersection of The Diamond and The Causeway. (Unilever Collections, Unilever Art, Archives and Records Management, Port Sunlight)

Fig. 24 The Diamond, 1911. Looking N to the site of the Lady Lever Art Gallery. Roads have been laid out in accordance with Prestwich's plan; on the L is the re-sited gymnasium (cf. Fig. 16) with swimming bath beyond; the small classical bandstand (Lomax Simpson, 1905–1906) has also been moved in connection with the replanning, having originally been built further N; a circle in the centre of the intersection with The Causeway is where the war memorial now stands. A new street lamp may be seen already in place (cf. Fig. 71). (*Progress*, vol. 11, 1911, p. 129)

Fig. 25 The Diamond. Looking N to Lady Lever Art Gallery (W. & S. Owen, 1913–22); cottages (Lomax Simpson, 1911–13) in Queen Mary's Drive (L) and King George's Drive (R); cottages shown immediately to R of art gallery were never built. (T. Raffles Davison, *Port Sunlight*, 1916, p. 12)

forces' volunteers, included shell manufacture as well as the enhanced supply of glycerine – a vital part of armament production.) It thus invites some comparison with the estates built at the same time by the Ministry of Munitions such as Well Hall and Gretna. Further housing was built on the Bromborough Port Estate and Lever formed an independent company to develop this to an overall plan initially designed by himself. With its provision for vast new areas of industry (as well as housing) and with sites not restricted to Lever companies, it followed on from Trafford Park and Slough to become a forerunner of 1930s trading estates such as the Team Valley estate in Gateshead. With continuing growth of production, including the opening of a new margarine factory on the Bromborough estate, seaborne imports, particularly of palm oil, grew quickly (Lever had established his own shipping line as early as 1916, one of the antecedents of the later Palm Line), and a large private dock was constructed on the Mersey foreshore for seagoing vessels. Opened in 1931, it was at the time the largest private dock in the United Kingdom. Later activity included the building of some of the caissons for the Mulberry harbours in the Second World War. Its eventual post-war decline led to it being filled in and its site now forms part of the thirty-hectare Port Sunlight Riverside Park, opened in 2014, whose planting can be seen terminating the vista along Bolton Road.

Both Woodhead and Bromborough include cottage blocks by Lomax Simpson as well as Cleland & Hayward, awarded in competition, with the blocks generally limited to a number of attractive but fairly economical standard designs (Figs 26–28). Elsewhere, isolated groups of additional houses were also built on Old Chester Road and The Wiend, but these remained physically separate from the village proper. Land was also acquired on Old Chester Road for the village recreation ground, whose stadium featured so prominently in the 1981 David Puttnam film *Chariots of Fire*. Within Port Sunlight itself, approximately 890 houses had been completed by the time of Lever's death in 1925, few of them later than 1911. Some resumption of activity was initiated in his lifetime, for building work by Lomax Simpson, immediately west of the art gallery, is of 1924–26. It included the opening up of a short vista aligned on the gallery, involving the demolition of some earlier cottages, as well as the building of new, and the layout provided a setting for the later Leverhulme Memorial (Figs 29–31).

The development of the main lines of the village ends with the building of a terraced garden and monumental arch. Dating from 1933–34, by Lomax Simpson, these terminate the south continuation of The Diamond and help compensate for the absence of the public buildings of Prestwich's plan. Further cottages were also added in the 1930s, including Jubilee Crescent of 1938, commemorating the fiftieth anniversary of foundation (Fig. 32). The village suffered general damage in the Second World War, with the complete loss of the Collegium and

Fig. 26 Port Sunlight in 1917 showing housing on the Woodhead Estate immediately east of New Chester Road. The development was stimulated by the wartime needs of the factory and initially conceived as an extension of the village. Its houses were later sold off. Within the village proper in place of the radiating street pattern adjoining Christ Church proposals for extending the churchyard and for houses east of the school are shown, neither of which were undertaken. The future site for the war memorial is indicated. (Gavin Hunter)

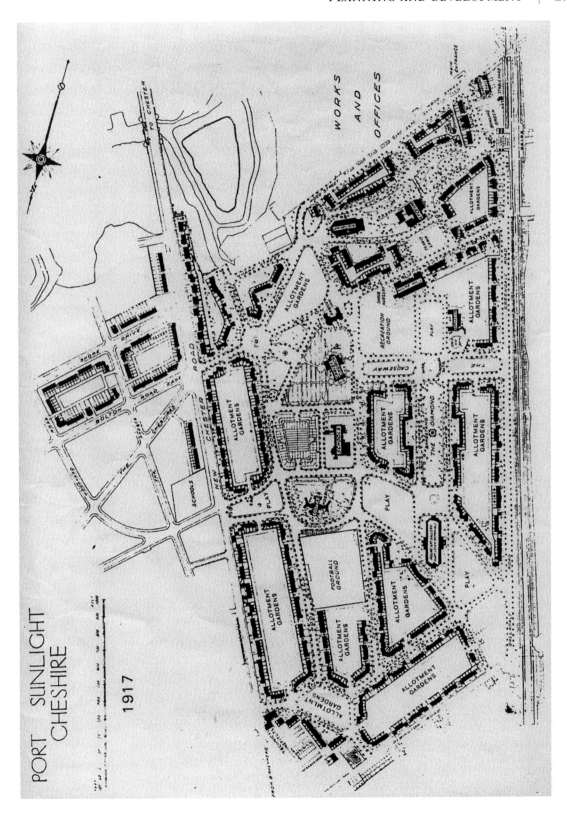

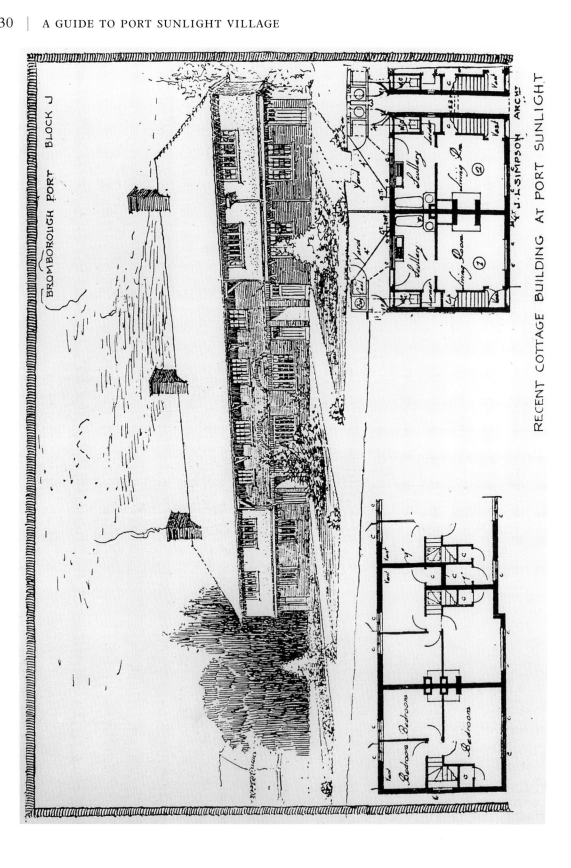

RECENT COTTAGE BUILDING AT PORT SUNLIGHT

Fig. 27 Proposed block of six houses designed for Bromborough and Woodhead estates by J. Lomax Simpson, one of a number of standard designs. (*The Builder*, 2 November 1917)

Fig. 28 The 'Bromboro Port Estate' development as envisaged in a promotional brochure of c. 1930. Port Sunlight seen bottom left with the New Chester Road running north–south immediately above on the plan. The original coloured version of this drawing shows sites allotted for

housing continuously bordering the east side of New Chester Road. Lever's original scheme for the development of Bromborough had envisaged a series of diagonal roads superimposed onto a grid of new residential avenues, but only a small part of this was built, and by the time of this publication much of the area was now allotted to industry. The earlier Price's model village of 1853 can be seen on the other side of New Chester Road from Port Sunlight. (*Bromboro Port Estate, c. 1930*)

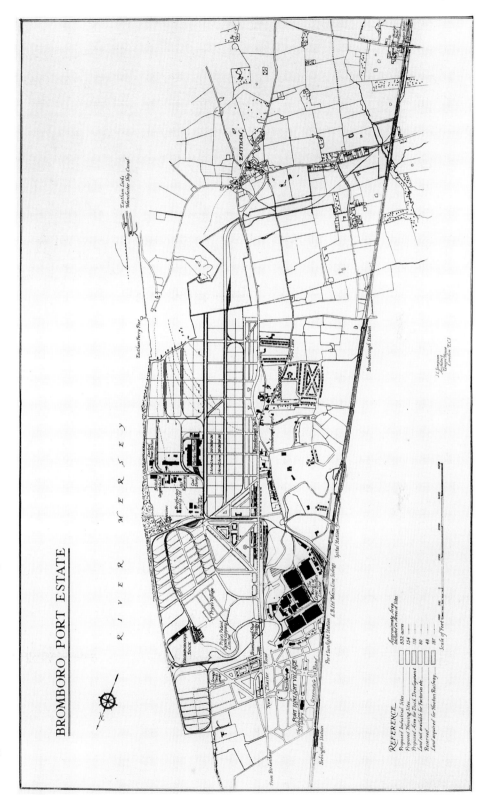

BROMBORO PORT ESTATE

REFERENCE

Approximately Area
Included in Area of Sites

Proposed Industrial Sites .... 552 acres
New Pool Site 154
Proposed Area for Dock Development 118
Land not available for Development 80
Reserved 48
Land acquired for Wootton Railway 187

Scale of Feet

Fig. 29 Windy Bank, junction with The Diamond before the building of the Lady Lever Art Gallery. This postcard view is one of a number of the village produced by Lever Brothers illustrating various aspects of Port Sunlight and its buildings. Seen here are Nos. 12-18 Windy Bank (Grayson & Ould), in one of which, No. 14, H. Bloomfield Bare organised an arts and crafts studio during 1903–1905. Cottages in the distance were partially rebuilt or demolished 1924–26 to facilitate the formation of the new approach to the gallery from Greendale Road. (Unilever Collections, Unilever Art, Archives and Records Management, Port Sunlight)

Windy Bank, Port Sunlight.

Fig. 30 Windy Bank. Looking E to Leverhulme Memorial and Lady Lever Art Gallery. The axial vista opened up by Lomax Simpson, c. 1924–26. On L the side of No. 10 Greendale Road, Nos. 1–3 Windy Bank, and part of No. 5, which links up with Nos. 17–22 Queen Mary's Drive. (Unilever Collections, Unilever Art, Archives and Records Management, Port Sunlight)

Fig. 31 Leverhulme Memorial, in front of W entrance of Lady Lever Art Gallery. Completed 1930; designed by J. Lomax Simpson; sculpture by (Sir) W. Reid Dick.

(Unilever Collections, Unilever Art, Archives and Records Management, Port Sunlight)

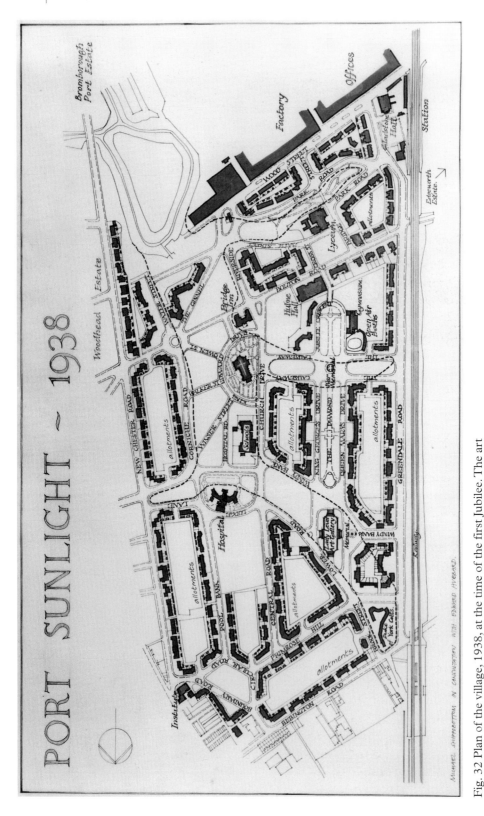

Fig. 32 Plan of the village, 1938, at the time of the first Jubilee. The art gallery has been completed and the formal vista cut through between it and the railway (see Fig. 27), involving demolition of some cottages (cf. Fig. 20); a formal termination has been given to the S end of The Diamond, and Jubilee Crescent erected in it; other buildings added since 1914 include Duke of York Cottages at the NW (bottom LH) corner; the war memorial stands at the central intersection. (Drawn by Michael Shippobottom in consultation with Edward Hubbard)

shops on Bridge Street. A number of houses were destroyed on Boundary Road, Pool Bank and Bridge Street, with many resulting casualties.

In 1960 Port Sunlight was placed under the management of Unilever Merseyside Ltd (a Unilever services company renamed UML Ltd in 1968). In a modernisation programme carried out by the Estates Department of the company from 1963, cottages were comprehensively renovated (see p. 43) and within the superblock enclosures allotments were replaced by garages and new gardens. Closure of some roads has banished unnecessary through traffic, and with Dutch elm disease having taken disastrous toll, a scheme of landscape rejuvenation was put in hand. This extended over a period of ten years, following the appointment of Pirkko Higson & Associates of Milton Keynes as consultants in 1978. Attention was given to resurfacing of paved areas, as well as to providing extensive and imaginatively varied planting, with tree planting concentrated in The Causeway and The Diamond. The roads are maintained by the local authority, to whom inappropriate and obtrusive street lamps belong.

The most fundamental development within Port Sunlight's first century was social rather than visual, for in 1980 cottages began to be made available for tenants to purchase. Protected by restrictive covenants as well as listed building and conservation area legislation, some two-thirds of the village cottages have been sold on the open market, with occupation no longer restricted to company employees. A Heritage Centre was opened in 1984 in the former library on Greendale Road, but was later transferred to the former Girls' Club, now renamed the

Fig. 33 War Memorial, Sir William Goscombe John (1916–21), commemorating the lives of 512 Lever Brothers employees who died in the First World War, with names of casualties from the Second World War added on the plinth beneath. General view with the end of King George's Drive far left and Christ Church (W. & S. Owen, 1902–1904) far right. (Mark Watson)

Museum, in 2006. To meet the needs of an ageing population, proposals for a new sheltered housing scheme on a site between Central Road and Pool Bank, designed by the local practice, Paddock Johnson Partnership, were implemented in 1999, but controversial plans for housing on Wharf Street, designed initially to echo the character of the factory, were temporarily halted because of local opposition.

Following on from this, the Port Sunlight Village Trust (PSVT), a registered charity, was established by Unilever in 1999 to secure the future of the village. PSVT's mission statement emphasises that the Trust is the guardian 'of a unique and beautiful village working with its community to ensure a great quality of life for residents and to celebrate William Lever's amazing legacy through cultural and learning experiences for all'. PSVT now looks after some 290 houses and flats – most of the main public buildings together with the Port Sunlight Museum – and it maintains the extensive landscape. Its achievements are impressive, with several key buildings and monuments extensively repaired in recent years, including the War Memorial and Hesketh Hall, which has been well restored externally and converted into apartments, as also have Nos. 17–21 Bolton Road. Additionally, the Trust is undertaking innovative trials of cottages for use in historical displays and holiday letting. No less impressive has been the implementation of a tree-planting and tree-replacement policy (there are some 1,350 trees in the village) and the publishing of guiding policy documentation for the village and landscape as a whole, notably in the form of Conservation Plans, which lay out policies for the future for all to see.

Further developments in the village include the building of the Philip Leverhulme Apartments (named after Lever's grandson) on the site of an earlier nondescript 1960s industrial training block and the erection of new housing on Water Street, Woodhead Row by Paddock Johnson Partnership, reflecting the Port Sunlight character, yet looking of its date. More sheltered housing on a perimeter brownfield site on Wharf Street has followed in 2015. The majority of this new work is sited away from the main village areas so that it is still possible to visit the village and see little change in its appearance since Lever's time.

Notes
1 Information from Gavin Hunter.
2 W. H. Lever, *The Buildings Erected at Port Sunlight and Thornton Hough*, 1902; 2nd edn, 1905.
3 *Liverpool Post*, 13 August 1923.
4 Margaret Stansgate, *My Exit Visa*, 1992, p. 103.
5 *Visit of International Housing Conference to Port Sunlight*, pamphlet, 1907, pp. 10–11.
6 I am grateful to Gavin Hunter for information on these associated estates.

Housing and Architectural Character

The visual harmony of the village may give the impression that the house designs were produced to a consistent policy of appointing architects, but prior to 1910 this was not the case. Quite apart from the changes and additions made to the original plan of the village as it grew, the way architects were selected, at least until 1910, was subject to changing approaches. After the first houses had been designed by William Owen, the next phase of work was the result of a limited competition, with Grayson & Ould and Douglas & Fordham involved, as well as possibly others. The phase also included a village shop and what became the Gladstone Hall. Later blocks in the early part of the village include work by T. M. Lockwood, Huon A. Matear and J. J. Talbot. In the great burst of activity following the opening of the Victoria Bridge and the building of Greendale Road, the established group of architects was joined by Edmund Kirby, H. Beswick, Pain and Blease, T. T. Rees and Lever's closest friend Jonathan Simpson, who had not been involved before. Until now, only north-western architects had been used, but, around 1897–99, Lever deliberately invited a group of London-based architects to contribute designs: these were Edwin Lutyens, Ernest George & Yeates, Maurice B. Adams and Ernest Newton. Their blocks were mixed in with work by the others and are not markedly superior. According to Lomax Simpson, William Curtis Green was also invited but confirmation of this has always been lacking. However, there remains one block, 25–27 Windy Bank/14–16 Church Drive, whose architect has yet to be properly identified. Could this be an early work by Green?

The Kirby Archive confirms that Lever liked to keep some designs to hand in order to be ready to build as required, so it is possible that definitive sites were not always known at the time of design. However, as against the seemingly random distribution of blocks by different architects along such roads as Greendale and New Chester Roads, around 1902, 1905 and again 1906/07, Grayson & Ould were employed for groups of four to five houses – on the north side of Boundary Road, at the north end of Pool Bank and at the junction of Greendale Road (the last subsequently drastically remodelled for the new formal western approach to the Art Gallery). Lever held a competition in 1904/05 for houses around Pool Bank and Central Road, open to architects or assistants who were members of the Liverpool Architectural Society, for groups of seven and five cottages: C. E. Deacon & Horsburgh were awarded first prize and, in a special category for architectural assistants, the award was given to William Naseby Adams (c. 1887–1952), then still a pupil of Reilly. A surviving unexecuted design by the Liverpool architect Herbert J. Rowse, another of Reilly's protégés, and also for a site on Central Road, may well have been submitted for the same competition as also may be a published design by F. I. M. Owen. But the competition was perhaps unusual, as in 1905, in inviting Bradshaw & Gass to design a group of cottages, Lever categorically stated that 'we do not put Architects, however, in competition one with the other, so that no two architects prepare plans in competition for the same site'.[1] Others involved at this time were Ormrod and Pomeroy; Lever's close friend from Liverpool University, Charles Reilly; H. Bloomfield Bare, and Garnet, Wright and Garnet, with F. J. Barnish. No housing at all was built in 1907 and any building work in progress then was halted – owing to the adverse impact of the *Daily Mail* libel case. Thereafter, only a few blocks were built – for example, the two by F. J. Barnish on Central Road and the three by W. & S. Owen in Water Street – before Lomax Simpson took over in 1910 on appointment as the company architect. In a similar fashion, various local north-western contractors were involved in building the early cottages and factory, including Richard Beckett, brother-in-law to the architect John Douglas, and Robert Neil and Sons, perhaps the largest regional firm of contractors at the time, but later building work was generally handled by Lever Brothers' own building department.

The era in which Port Sunlight was conceived was a golden age of English domestic architecture. The influence of William Morris and the Arts & Crafts movement, and the refinement and sensitivity of Late Victorian aestheticism took their place in the new relaxed and confident 'domestic revival'. Free and eclectic adaptations of historical precedent prevailed, but particular impetus came from the styles of south-eastern vernacular building traditions as interpreted by George Devey and by W. Eden Nesfield and R. Norman Shaw. The 'Old English' manner of Nesfield and Shaw (to use their own term) and their followers was marked by picturesque groupings and varying materials artfully deployed. It is much in evidence at Port Sunlight, but inspired by the north-west rather than the Home Counties. Style and character were confined to external display, cottage interiors being on the whole utilitarian (Fig. 34), though the larger houses had grander panelled doors, simple moulded cornices and more elaborate fire surrounds. Advice on decorating and furnishing simple rooms, given in the *Sunlight Yearbook* (1898), may perhaps have been aimed at tenants, and Lever was interested to show that even simple interiors could be attractive and well fitted out – for example, offering prizes in 1919 to the Bolton Municipal School of Arts for the best designs of cottage bedrooms and living rooms. The backs also are plain, in contrast to the costly front elevations (Figs 11, 35, 37).

No two blocks of cottages are identical, giving to the village the variety which is one of its endearing qualities. Owen's earliest cottages of 1889–90 are simple, with one block merely a plain brick rectangle with shallow oriels, though others are relieved by tile-hung gables. Greater ambition marks the work by Owen, Grayson & Ould and Douglas & Fordham which immediately followed. With much half-timbering, carved wood-work and masonry, pargetting (ornamental plasterwork), moulded and twisted chimneys, and leaded glazing patterns, it established not only a penchant for display, but also the high quality of external materials and detailing which was to be a hallmark of virtually all subsequent building in the village. The early work is mostly hard and crisp, with, for instance, timber framing and render set off by glowing Ruabon brick and glazed terracotta. Showing the influence of William Morris and John Ruskin, the exposed framing was proudly described by both Lever and Lomax Simpson as being of solid beam and frame construction – not simply applied decorative boards. The judicious and effective use of red pressed brick (not now universally accepted as an attractive material) is seen to particular advantage in the 1889–97 portion. In contrast are the softer and mellow textures of much of the twentieth-century development. Especially apparent in the buildings of The Diamond, these illustrate the sensitivity to materials typical of the Arts & Crafts movement's Edwardian phase. Though picturesque vernacular always prevailed, a further twentieth-century (post-1913) element may be discerned in a neat and urbane underlying classicism, not specifically Neo-Georgian, but affined to it.

More subtle changes in the twentieth century are apparent in the decorative schemes. It is generally agreed that the blackening of timber frames, which is now such a characteristic practice in the north-west and west midlands, known generally as 'black and white', dates from the very late eighteenth century onwards, arising from then newly available access to coal tar products. But architects like Edward Ould and Lomax Simpson admired the traditional finish of natural oak and at Port Sunlight it is clear that much, if not all, of the timber framing on houses was initially left in its natural state. Certainly, much of Lomax Simpson's work was only blackened, and without his knowledge, after the Second World War. Another change too is the present variety of colour schemes on the cottages which has developed in the twentieth century (along with the adoption of brilliant white paint), and it would seem a simpler and more muted paint scheme was implemented initially: W. L. George refers to the general use of green paint on doors and window frames – echoes of which perhaps survive today in the dark green paint used on joinery throughout the rear service yard areas, though this may not have been fully comprehensive; in the case of, for example, 30–38 Primrose Hill, its external woodwork was described in a contemporary account as being 'purply–grey'. Similarly rendered decorative panels were

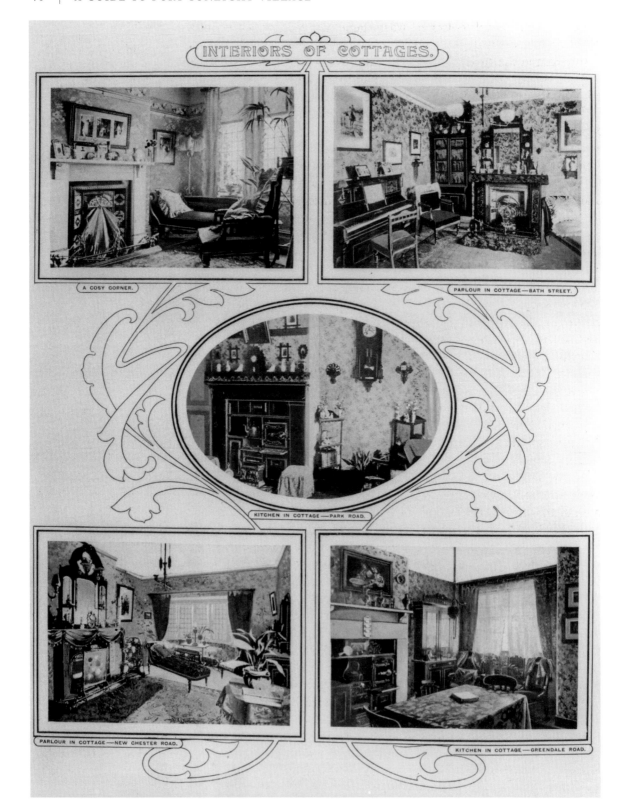

INTERIORS OF COTTAGES.

A COSY CORNER.

PARLOUR IN COTTAGE—BATH STREET.

KITCHEN IN COTTAGE—PARK ROAD.

PARLOUR IN COTTAGE—NEW CHESTER ROAD.

KITCHEN IN COTTAGE—GREENDALE ROAD.

initially given a weak coloured wash, generally picking out moulded details in a gentle way.

Inherent in the variety and elaboration was the danger of an exhibition-like quality, and Lever wisely abandoned an idea for groups of cottages in styles representing countries in which Lever Brothers had factories. Nevertheless a block in avowedly Belgian style (by Grayson & Ould) was built (Fig. 40). In fact, the stylistic diversity is not as great as has sometimes been made out. Despite variations of form, design elements, detail, and the nature and colour of materials and finishes, the cottages are, with few exceptions, within the broad framework of vernacular revival idiom. This, together with a common scale, to say nothing of the guiding hand of Lever, provided a unifying factor and made for harmony. The personalities of individual architects seldom obtrude. Indeed, it is difficult to distinguish from each other the respective works of those habitually employed.

One block of cottages (by Kirby, now demolished) was a reproduction of Shakespeare's birthplace, and another (by Talbot) was closely based on the timber-framed Kenyon Peel Hall in Lancashire (Fig. 41), but such literal historicism was exceptional, and many of the blocks are of considerable originality and resourcefulness. Even the more inventive and fanciful are for the most part carefully and soberly done, with light-heartedness seldom tending to whimsy, and the general standard of design is consistently high.

Even so, Port Sunlight was never the pioneer in terms of architecture that it was within the social and planning fields, and early-twentieth-century advanced thought demanded a more restrained approach. In 1915 the *Builder* criticised cottages of 1906 by Bradshaw & Gass as 'over-featured', and in 1898 the *British Architect* had praised Newton's, built at that time, for their simplicity. Lever was aware that lavishness had drawbacks, commenting in 1902 that '[the] tendency at Port Sunlight has been during the last few years for our architects to become more and more elaborate in architectural design, and more and more extravagant in the use of costly building material'.[2] While approving the results of what could be done with unlimited money, he conceded the greater usefulness of achieving satisfactory ends with economy of means. Lever encouraged the use of new and cheaper building techniques elsewhere, (p. 81) but at Port Sunlight remained faithful to embellishment and traditional skills. Even the simpler of Lomax Simpson's post-1910 cottages have delightful touches of ornament.

The blocks throughout the village range in size from two to eighteen cottages, though most consist of between three and ten. Many are of irregular plan, set back to form greens, ingeniously turning corners, or otherwise responding to site conditions and restrictions. Even if not progressive, architectural style accorded with good contemporary work. Similarly, domestic accommodation was to the accepted standard for

Fig. 34 Cottage interiors, c. 1901. (W. H. Lever, *The Buildings Erected at Port Sunlight and Thornton Hough*, 2nd edn, 1905, p. 24)

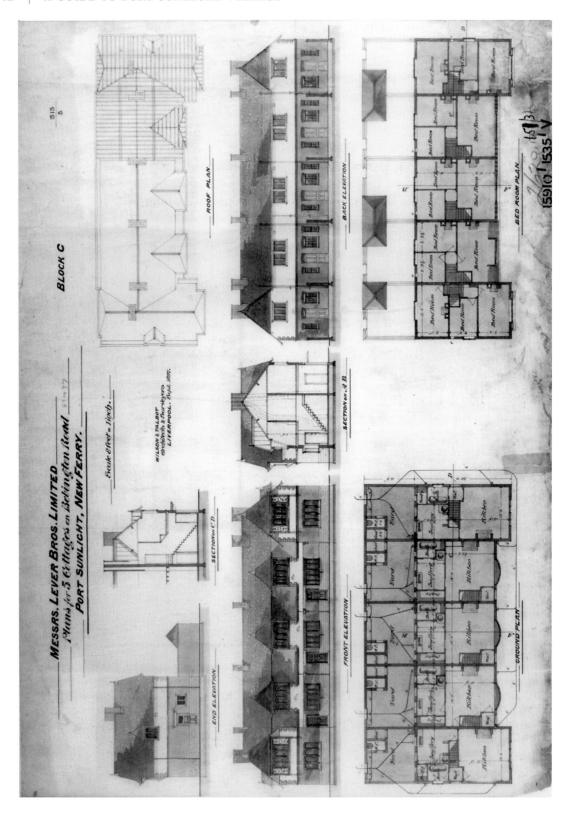

working-class model housing of the day, with only the provision of bath-rooms being remarkable. Detailed planning varies from one house or block to another, but accommodation was of two standard types: the Kitchen Cottage, with kitchen, scullery and larder and three bedrooms above (Figs 31, 32), and the Parlour Cottage with, in addition, a parlour and fourth bedroom (Figs 33–35 and Fig. 8). A WC was reached from outside and it was noted that 'each house has the exceptional luxury of a bathroom'.[3] Some, though, had merely a covered bath in the scullery, and most bathrooms were at ground-floor level. Certain cottages had less than the standard accommodation; some of the four-bedroomed type were intended as clerks' houses, and a few larger houses were built for managerial staff. In 1929, installation began of electric lighting to replace gas.

Air-raid damage was suffered in the Second World War and, under the direction of Lomax Simpson, most cottages affected were faithfully restored or completely rebuilt in external facsimile, at least on the main frontages.

Unilever's modernisation work commenced in 1963 and continued in progressive phases for some twenty years, a little-celebrated, pioneering village conservation scheme. Not only did it bring garages,

Fig. 35 Nos. 89–97 Bebington Road (Wilson & Talbot, 1897–99). Example of the three-bedroomed 'Kitchen Cottage' type. Architect's drawing. (Unilever Collections, Unilever Art, Archives and Records Management, Port Sunlight)

Fig. 36 Nos. 89–97 Bebington Road. Photograph c. 1902. (Unilever Collections, Unilever Art, Archives and Records Management, Port Sunlight)

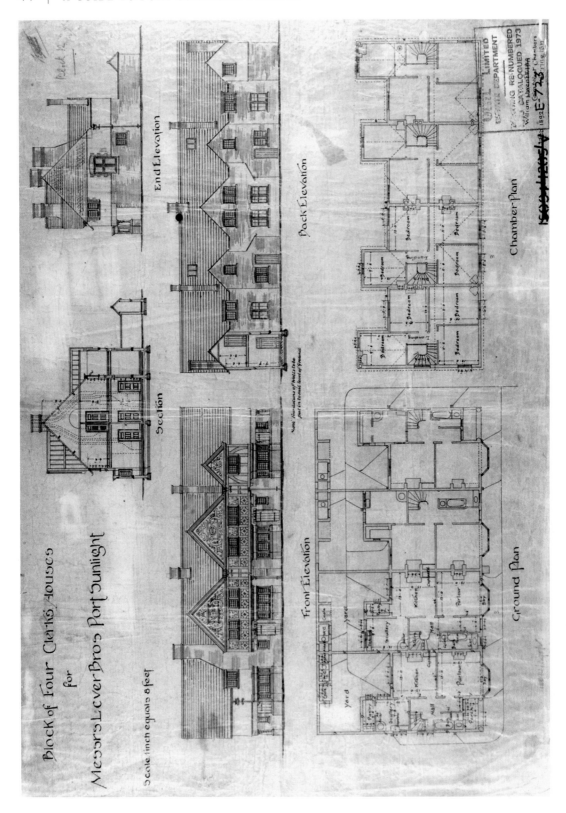

Fig. 37 Nos. 1–7 Park Road (Owen, 1892). Example of the four-bedroomed 'Parlour Cottage' type. Architect's drawing. (Unilever Collections, Unilever Art, Archives and Records Management, Port Sunlight)

Fig. 38 No. 5 Park Road, pargetted gable. (Unilever Collections, Unilever Art, Archives and Records Management, Port Sunlight)

Fig. 39 N side of Park Road. Nos. 1–7 and Nos. 9–17 (Owen, 1892). (Colin Jackson)

Fig. 40 'Belgian Cottages'. Nos. 23–24 Windy Bank (Grayson & Ould, 1907). Built in Flemish style, of bricks imported from Belgium. (Unilever Collections, Unilever Art, Archives and Records Management, Port Sunlight)

Fig. 41 Kenyon Peel Cottages, Nos. 11–17 Greendale Road (Talbot, 1902). A close but not exact copy of the now demolished Kenyon Peel Hall, Lancashire. (Mark Watson)

but cottages were renovated and, with some skill, internally remodelled and refitted to modern standards. Some units were combined together, rear elevations were adapted, and extensions added, but with minimal alteration of frontages, though marred by the removal of some leaded light glazing and removal of some chimney pots.

Less happy have been the various rear extensions, conservatories and picture windows introduced by individual residents following purchase of houses. Yet with the frontages preserved to an exemplary degree, and the layout little changed since the death of the founder, Port Sunlight offers a unique opportunity to experience – and enjoy – a complete environment expressing late-nineteenth- and early-twentieth-century social and visual ideals.

Notes

1 Jane and Timothy Linguard, *Bradshaw Gass & Hope*, 2007, p. 88.
2 W. H. Lever, *The Buildings Erected at Port Sunlight and Thornton Hough*, 1st edition, 1902, p. 9.
3 *Building News*, vol. 76, 1899, p. 60.

Fig. 42 Nos. 38-48 Park Road (T. M. Lockwood, 1895). Showing timber framing in original state and with leaded lights to the windows. (Historic England Archives)

5

Public Buildings

'Few self-contained communities are richer than Port Sunlight in social and educational institutions and in buildings to house them.'[1] Lever believed in providing a wide range of facilities, and gave encouragement to the numerous cultural, sporting and other societies and organisations which flourished from an early date (when the village was comparatively isolated from other amenities). He criticised the Well Hall Estate at Woolwich, built for munition workers, because community buildings were lacking, and no such criticism could be levelled at Port Sunlight.

Some served dual or multi-purpose roles from the start; most have undergone changes of use, either as additional buildings were erected, or as requirements and social patterns changed, and there have been many enlargements and structural alterations. Similar architectural idiom marks both housing and public buildings, and a distinctive feature of many of the latter had been hanging signs carried by sturdy timber posts, well suited to the village (Fig. 46). In 1988 replacements of very different character began to appear. Though the standard of maintenance of the village as a whole remains extremely high, leasing of certain buildings to outside bodies means that immaculate perfection is no longer universal.

THE GLADSTONE HALL (William Owen, 1891, Fig. 43) (the opening ceremony was performed by the statesman) was the first assembly and recreation hall. It also served as a men's dining room (planned with smaller rooms for male and female clerks respectively to take their meals) until canteen facilities were provided in the factory in 1910 (Fig. 44). Lever frequently lectured there; concerts of sacred music were held on Sunday evenings, and with stage facilities successively improved, it is now called the Gladstone Theatre. A functional and economical structure, it was described by Lever as 'the most appropriate Village Hall we have. It is simple and unpretentious, admirably adapted for the purpose for which it was designed, and most suitable and appropriate for erection in a village.'[2]

Like the Gladstone Hall, a VILLAGE SHOP (by Grayson & Ould) of 1891 resulted from the competition held in that year. It forms an appealing half-timbered termination to an attached row of cottages. It became the Post Office (since 2001 a tea room) (Fig. 45) when, with the growth of the village, it was superseded by three shops (Douglas & Fordham, 1894) run by company employees themselves on co-operative lines. The first floor above them, later known as the COLLEGIUM,

Fig. 43 Gladstone Theatre, originally Gladstone Hall (Owen, 1891), with later additions of backstage facilities and porch, by J. Lomax Simpson. (Mark Watson)

Fig. 44 Gladstone Hall in use as men's dining hall, 1895. Unlike Hulme Hall, built ten years later, its kitchen facilities were limited and meals were not served – note luncheon baskets. Paintings from Lever's collection adorn the walls and Hawarden Castle (Gladstone's country residence) is depicted on the stage curtain. (Unilever Collections, Unilever Art, Archives and Records Management, Port Sunlight)

was built as a Girls' Institute – a club more educational than social. The block was destroyed by bombing and not rebuilt. By the same architects and of similar date is the DELL BRIDGE (1894) and the building known originally as THE SCHOOLS (1894–96, enlarged 1898) (Fig. 9). This was also used for Sunday services before the church was built, and was available for other functions on week-nights. 'All the social work of the village,' said Lever in 1902, 'centres round these buildings', which he described as those 'of which we are most proud at Port Sunlight, both architecturally and otherwise'.[3] It was the most important building to have been added to the village at its date, and forms a visual focal point in the early portion. Until the 1902 Education Act, the schools were run by the company, and after later becoming redundant for local authority requirements, the building served as a Staff Training College and was renamed the Lyceum. It has since been put to a number of various uses and is now offices and a Social Club.

Two buildings of 1896, of more domestic scale, completed the series of institutions provided in the early portion. The Men's SOCIAL CLUB (by Grayson & Ould), first called the Pavilion, has had several names and is now the Lever Club. After an attempt to run a Girls' Hostel proved a failure, the building erected for this purpose (by Maxwell & Tuke, Fig. 46) was put to a bewildering number of uses within a short space

Fig. 45 Currently a tea room but earlier the Post Office and originally a general store (Grayson & Ould, 1891). (T. Raffles Davison, *Port Sunlight*, 1916, Pl. 19)

Fig. 46 Former Girls' Hostel (Maxwell & Tuke, 1896), later Heritage Centre and National Westminster Bank, now offices and bank. Shown when used as Lever Library; early-twentieth-century hanging sign suspended from timber post no longer exists and this record of it may be compared with replacements. (T. Raffles Davison, *Port Sunlight*, 1916, Pl. 17)

of time before being partially occupied, from 1903, by the Lever Free Library and Museum, a precursor of the Lady Lever Art Gallery. Later in use as a Heritage Centre, now offices and a bank. Anxious that employees' wages be paid into individual accounts, Lever first invited a bank to occupy the premises in 1919.

HULME HALL (William & Segar Owen, 1900–1901, Figs 47, 48), though from the start used for special functions and gatherings, was built specifically as a girls' dining room, to seat 1500, and with kitchens for the service of meals. With canteens established in the factory, it served as a museum and art gallery, and Lever considered enlarging it for this purpose, before deciding to build the Lady Lever Art Gallery. It was at Hulme Hall in 1914 that, by remote control and the use of a model, King George V laid the foundation stone of the new gallery. Hulme Hall's stylish exterior is thoroughgoing and consistently done, even if no more elaborate than the Port Sunlight norm. However, moulded and enriched plaster-work marks high interior standards, and Lever clearly thought things had gone far enough when in developing his comments on extravagant construction (see p. 41), he compared the Gladstone and Hulme Halls, to the detriment of the latter, remarking that it shows 'what can be done with unlimited money lavishly spent, which is perhaps the least useful lesson village architecture should teach'.[4]

Fig. 47 Hulme Hall (W. & S. Owen, 1900–1901). Built as women's dining hall. (Colin Jackson)

Fig. 48 Hulme Hall under construction. Photograph 1900. (Unilever Collections, Unilever Art, Archives and Records Management, Port Sunlight)

Fig. 49 Bridge Inn (Grayson & Ould, 1900). Entrance (S) front, before glazing of verandahs and building of porch. (T. Raffles Davison, *Port Sunlight*, 1916, Pl. 24)

The Bridge Inn (Grayson & Ould, 1900, Figs 18–20, 49) similarly shows no sign of stinting, but is simpler in treatment, and Lever seems to have thought that he here received better value for money. Named after the now-vanished Victoria Bridge, this idealised evocation of an ancient hostelry had dining, tea and assembly rooms, and a few guest bedrooms. It began as a temperance hotel, but after a couple of years a deputation requested that a licence be applied for. Although it was against his wishes, Lever complied, after having put the matter to the vote in a poll of village residents, and in 1903 the Bridge Inn was taken over by the Liverpool Public House Trust Co. This was a branch of Earl Grey's Public House Trust, a body which, with its circumspect serving of drink, was viewed with suspicion by the licensing trade. Having failed to secure adequate returns, the Trust relinquished responsibility, which was assumed in 1905 by a committee representing residents and Lever Brothers. A successor committee and a period of direct management by UML were followed by the granting of a lease to a brewery company in 1981. It was sold in 2002.

More was undertaken in 1902. Reflecting Lever's concern for physical fitness, in that year William & Segar Owen built the gymnasium and an open-air swimming bath (Figs 17, 89). The former (later the Boys' Club) was a weather-boarded building which, in accordance with Prestwich's plan, was moved in 1910 from its original site to adjoin the swimming bath. It later became a Mac Fisheries store. Both are now destroyed. Except for the church, the most notable building of this period architecturally is the Technical Institute (J. J. Talbot, 1902–1903, almost immediately extended by Grayson and Ould, 1904–1905), later Hesketh Hall and home of the Port Sunlight branch of the Royal British Legion (Fig. 50). It was converted into fourteen apartments in 2014 by Paddock Johnson Architects, who undertook a skilful restoration of the exterior. The cost of the initial building was met, not by the company, but by Lever himself. By Grayson & Ould, also of 1902–03, are the large Church Drive schools (built originally to supplement the Douglas & Fordham building and leased to the local education authority). The schools are an important building nationally as 'They prefigured the neo-Georgian style which was soon to become widely used'.[5] The first stage of the Auditorium was also built at this time. This was an open-air theatre, its covered and fully equipped stage having a Renaissance-style proscenium (Fig. 90). Within a year or so the area was enclosed with canvas upon a light framework; this in turn gave way to a more solid structure, seating 3000, but it was never a success, and all has been demolished. Also by Grayson & Ould is the former Cottage Hospital (1905–1907), with early additions by Lomax Simpson and W. & S. Owen. The original wards were angled facing south and verandahs were later added. After use as a private nursing home, it became a technical training centre and then in 2006 it was converted into the Leverhulme

Fig. 50 Hesketh Hall, originally the Technical Institute (J. J. Talbot, 1902–1903). View shows the gables of the 1905 extension by Grayson & Ould. Converted to flats in 2014. The elaborately moulded, decorative render incorporates symbols and figures on themes of wisdom, learning and pleasure, with – in the gables – L. satyrs above cornucopia; R. putti supporting seahorse swags; and below – in the frieze – Christian symbolism and representations of relevant fables, with, for example, the hare and the tortoise; a pelican representing parental nurture, an owl for wisdom, a Liver bird or crane, a sailing ship, and the date 1905. (Mark Watson)

Fig. 51 Former Cottage Hospital (Grayson & Ould, 1905–1907). Later extended (*Progress*, vol. 6, 1905, p. 444); but following use as a nursing home, closed in 2002 and converted into the Leverhulme Hotel in 2008. Perspective by Roger Oldham, a Manchester based architect and illustrator.

Fig. 52 Former Residents' Club, originally Girls' Club (Lomax Simpson, 1913), and since 2006 the Port Sunlight Museum c. 1930. (Unilever Collections, Unilever Art, Archives and Records Management, Port Sunlight)

COTTAGE HOSPITAL PORT SUNLIGHT.

Hotel, for which use a number of sensitive additions have been made by Paddock Johnson using matching grey pebbledash and Westmorland slate (Fig. 51). Later, in 1913, came the Girls' Club (later Residents' Club) which Lomax Simpson skilfully handled opposite the site which had already been chosen for the art gallery (Fig. 52). It became the Port Sunlight Museum in 2006.

Christ Church and the Lady Lever Art Gallery (see p. 63) were built at the expense of Lever himself, and were his own special and personal contributions to the village. They express not a little of his ideals and philosophies. The church reflects his Nonconformity and his undemanding theology, combined with a love of medieval churches and of beauty and richness in architecture, and a desire for beauty and dignity in worship and liturgy. It was established as a non-denominational foundation, of a sort difficult to imagine outside the special circumstances and rarefied atmosphere of Port Sunlight. In fact its antecedents were rather on the interdenominational lines more familiar to a later generation, with the services which were held in the Schools being conducted in rotation by Free Church ministers and the vicar of New Ferry, in whose parish Port Sunlight lay. In 1900 the vicar withdrew from the scheme, and a resident minister for the village – a Wesleyan – was appointed. It was in his time that Christ Church was built. Though remaining non-denominational, it was vested by Lever in the

Fig. 53 Christ Church (W. & S. Owen, 1902–1904). (T. Raffles Davison, *Port Sunlight*, 1916, Pl. 30)

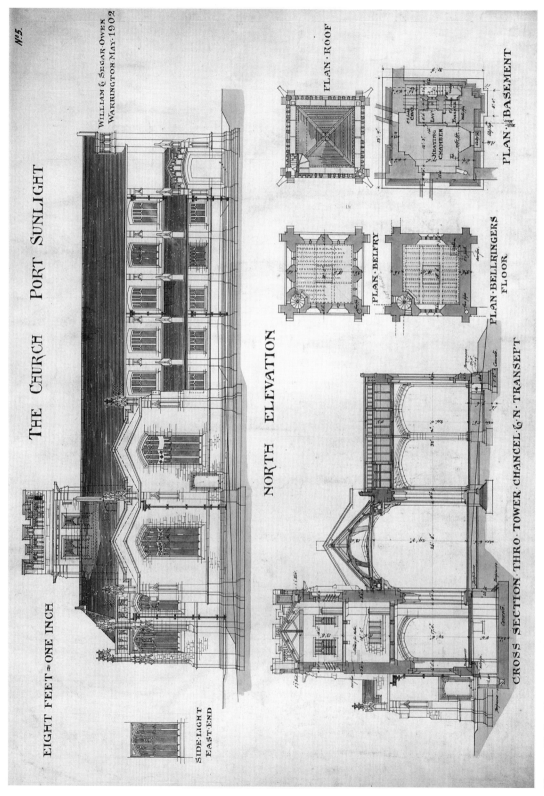

THE CHURCH PORT SUNLIGHT

WILLIAM & SEGAR OWEN
WARRINGTON MAY 1902

Nº 5.

PLAN · ROOF

PLAN · BASEMENT

PLAN · BELFRY

PLAN · BELLRINGERS
FLOOR

NORTH ELEVATION

EIGHT FEET = ONE INCH

SIDE·LIGHT
EAST·END

CROSS · SECTION · THRO · TOWER · CHANCEL · & · N · TRANSEPT

Fig. 54 Christ Church (W. & S. Owen, 1902–1904). Architect's drawing dated May 1902 showing north elevation, cross-section and tower plans. (National Museums Liverpool)

Congregational Union of England and Wales, with the stipulation that future ministers be Congregational. This was merely to ensure continuance and legal standing, but in 1972 Congregationalism took Christ Church into the United Reformed Church and it is no longer even officially non-denominational.

By William & Segar Owen and dating from 1902–1904, Christ Church (Figs 19, 20, 53–55) is of great splendour and sumptuousness. The style is the Neo-Perpendicular of the late phase of the Gothic Revival. It is built of red Cheshire sandstone with Arts & Crafts touches in its conventionalised features and details. Resembling work by Austin & Paley, it has all the quality and richness of the manner. The form is that of a parish church, with a long and fully fitted chancel, providing not a hint of Nonconformity. Despite the remarkable size and elaboration, an even grander scheme was first designed which Lever, to his lasting regret, rejected.

A structure to mark his future burial place and that of his wife, coterminous with the church, was designed soon after. In the form of a loggia and known as the Lady Lever Memorial, it was put in hand following her death in 1913 and contains an effigy by Sir William Goscombe John (Fig. 56). After Lever's own death, his effigy, by the same sculptor, was placed beside that of his wife.

Fig. 55 Christ Church. Detail of the roof trusses over the chancel. (Mark Watson)

Fig. 56 Christ Church. Lady Lever Memorial (W. & S. Owen, designed 1905, built 1913–14). Effigy by Sir W. Goscombe John, 1915. The drawing by T. Raffles Davison shows the loggia before the addition of Lever's own effigy and before the addition of railings, later infill of roof-lights and memorials to other Lever family members. (T. Raffles Davison, *Port Sunlight*, 1916, Pl. 33)

Fig. 57 War Memorial (Sir W. Goscombe John, 1916–21) SW view with upper group: Defence of the Home; lower group far right: The Royal Navy. (Mark Watson)

Other family members buried here are William Hulme Lever, the second Viscount Leverhulme (1888–1949) and his wife Winifred Agnes, Viscountess Leverhulme (1899–1966). An accompanying bust of the second Viscount, probably by Wheeler, was stolen in 2009.

Lever, whose taste in sculpture was progressive, was on terms of friendship with Goscombe John, an exponent of the naturalistic 'New Sculpture'. He was also responsible for the war memorial at the intersection of The Diamond and The Causeway, and it is one of his most successful works (Figs 33, 57). Lever conceived the idea and discussed it with him as early as 1916; models were shown at the Academy in 1919, and the completed work unveiled in 1921. It was at Lever's instigation that, after other possible locations had been considered, the war memorial was sited at the focal point of the village – a position which, it had been tacitly understood, was being reserved for a monument to himself. The Leverhulme Memorial of 1930 was therefore placed axially between the west front of the Lady Lever Art Gallery and the short vista which had been opened up c. 1924–26. With an obelisk designed by Lomax Simpson and sculpture by Sir William Reid Dick, it is a fine and worthy work, but in Port Sunlight superfluous. *Si monumentum requiris, circumspice.*

Notes

1 Viscount Leverhulme, *Viscount Leverhulme by his Son*, p. 89.
2 Lever, *The Buildings Erected at Port Sunlight and Thornton Hough*, 2nd edn, 1905, p. 10.
3 *Ibid.*, p. 14.
4 *Ibid.*, p. 12.
5 Malcolm Seaborne and Roy Lowe, *The English School: Its Architecture and Organisation*, vol. 2, 1870–1970, 1977, p. 24.

6

The Lady Lever Art Gallery

The centrepiece of the village today is the magnificent art gallery named after Lever's wife. It remains the only major public urban art gallery in Britain built by its founder to house the collection he had assembled for it, a practice much more common in America. Paradoxically, it was not conceived as a memorial to his wife, who died after design work on the gallery had already begun. The gallery, more than any other building, embodies Lever's strong belief in the power for good of art and good design-qualities, which had influenced him to develop Port Sunlight in the first place, and it marks the culmination of a series of museum and gallery projects which he had initiated. In 1899, Lever had purchased Hall i'th Wood, Bolton, a timber-framed medieval hall, and gifted it to the borough for use as a very early folk and technological museum.

Fig. 58 Lady Lever Art Gallery (W. & S. Owen, 1913–22), from SE. Photograph c. 1924. The foundation stone is immediately to the right of the entrance steps. Urns acquired from the Rothschild house, Aston Clinton. Boundary railings and planting now surround the gallery. The block of cottages of 1906 by Reilly is just visible far right but the later cottages by Lomax Simpson north-west of the gallery have clearly not yet been built. (Unilever Collections, Unilever Art, Archives and Records Management, Port Sunlight)

Within the village he had displayed pictures in the upper floor of the Girls' Hostel from 1903, the same year that he built the Music Room at Thornton Manor to display some of his collection, and, still later, from 1911, used the Hulme Hall for more comprehensive displays after the girls' dining use had been transferred into the factory. Although Lever was to be involved with many more museum/gallery projects later (for example, the gift of Lancaster House for use by the London Museum), it is the Lady Lever which will be remembered as his chief contribution in this field.

Fig. 60 Lady Lever Art Gallery. Main Hall, showing original black and white colour scheme. Photograph probably c. 1922. (Unilever Collections, Unilever Art, Archives and Records Management, Port Sunlight)

Fig. 59 Lady Lever Art Gallery under construction. Main Hall showing bare reinforced concrete structure. Photograph probably 1918. (British

Reinforced Concrete Engineering Company Ltd, *B.R.C. Structures*, 1927, p. 227; British Architectural Library/ RIBA)

Fig. 61 Proposed Art Gallery and Museum, Bolton. This accomplished perspective by Robert Atkinson of the Art Gallery and Museum proposed for Bolton's Queen's Park featured in Mawson's planning study for the town funded by Lever in 1910. The painting was exhibited at the Royal Academy and was used by Mawson as the frontispiece in his great *Civic Art* book of 1911. The Bolton Beautiful Scheme, as it was known, was also displayed at the influential RIBA Town Planning Conference and Exhibition of 1910. This powerful image clearly helped determine Lever's views on the nature of the new art gallery he was proposing for Port Sunlight itself.
(T. H. Mawson, *Bolton: A Study in Town Planning and Civic Art*, 1910)

The firm of William & Segar Owen was entrusted with the work, having initially prepared proposals for extending the Hulme Hall itself, Lomax Simpson being busy planning extensions to Thornton Manor and the Port Sunlight factory as well as much new housing in the village around The Diamond. The gallery was designed in 1913 and built 1914–22, with progress being delayed by the Great War. The structure is of reinforced concrete, then still unusual, if no longer pioneering, as a construction material. The British Reinforced Concrete Company built the shell, but the rest was undertaken by Lever Brothers' own Works Department (Bromborough Port Construction Company). Internal finishes and features were built up in plaster (Figs 59, 60) and the exterior clad in Portland stone. All stone carving was by Earp, Hobbs and Miller (successor firm to the great Victorian carver Thomas Earp) and J. J. Milson of Manchester. A warm air heating system was integrated with the structure, and the plant, by Killick & Cochran of Liverpool, had facilities which included washed canvas air filters which both cleaned the air and helped circulate cool air in hot weather. Equally advanced was the provision of individual picture lights – some seven years before the villagers benefited from electric lighting in their homes.

A chaste and lovely treasure box of a building, it is an essay in scholarly and accomplished beaux arts classicism, and, though the crowning glory of the village, it carried to extreme the departure into formality made by Prestwich's plan. Lever, who had been so impressed by the grandiose planning and architecture of the World's Fair twenty years before, continued to admire the classical movement in America and the comparable work of Professor Reilly and the Liverpool School of

Fig. 62 Lady Lever Art Gallery. Architect's drawing for E and W elevations. (National Museums Liverpool)

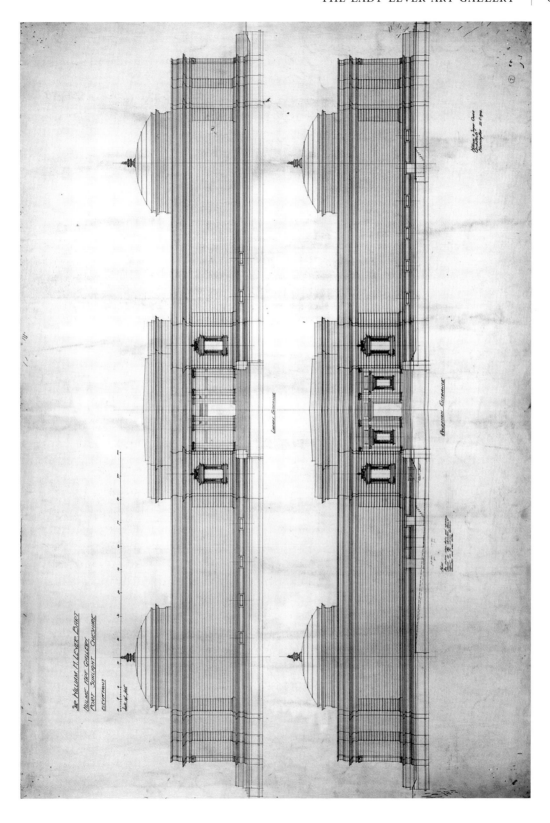

Architecture in Britain, an example of which was to feature prominently in Lever's own 1910 replanning scheme for Bolton, prepared by Mawson, which included a major new classical art gallery and museum (Fig. 61). This, coupled with his purchases from the McCulloch auction of 1913, clearly affected his thinking for the new gallery at Port Sunlight, both in terms of scale as well as style and siting – the gallery at Port Sunlight now being positioned to terminate the vista along The Diamond.

It was Lever who proposed the style and facing material. These were not, though, adopted without some misgivings, as witness a letter to Segar Owen:

> my suggestion of limestone and classical architecture must not be taken as ruling out all other styles. This was my first impression, but Mr Simpson [Lomax Simpson] has expressed the view, and I think he is probably right, that it would be a little too hard for Port Sunlight Village, and that Renaissance [i.e., an Early Renaissance], with red Runcorn stone would harmonise better with the Village. Please therefore feel at liberty to adopt whatever style you think best.

But Lever then showed Owen a photograph of an American gallery to aid their thoughts. Regrettably, the name of the gallery has not been recorded.[1]

Certainly, Lever wished to restrict the scale and height so as not to overwhelm nearby cottages, and it is a measure of the architects' skill that they minimised and successfully integrated the great bulk, giving it horizontal emphasis and articulating the windowless walls (which themselves speak of neoclassical purity and restraint), by concentrating interest at four Ionic entrances (Figs 25, 31, 58, 62). Greek Ionic (most elegant of all classical orders) is also used inside (Figs 60, 63).

The foundation stone was laid remotely by George V and Queen Mary in 1914, in a ceremony held in Hulme Hall, with the King pressing a button in the position of the future gallery on a model of the village (Fig. 68). The action of laying the stone was then repeated by a working model of the stone itself lowered into position by a model crane. This seemingly innovative arrangement, however, was not the only such example at the time: Edward VII had officially opened a Sanatorium in Montreal bearing his name, in 1909, by pressing a button at West Dean in Sussex, and the Lady Lever event was followed by similar 'remote' foundation stone ceremonies at, for example, the Caird Hall, Dundee, 10 July 1914 (just four months after the Lady Lever ceremony and also with George V and Queen Mary); the Freemasons' Hall, London, 1927; and the Birkenhead Central Library, 1934.

Lever himself conceived the basic layout of the plan and it has few major axes, so on paper is revealed as compartmentalised, lacking the spatial subtleties of true beaux arts expertise. Initially a library, with its own separate entrance, was intended; and a Masonic Room was

Fig. 63 Lady Lever Art Gallery. S Sculpture Hall.
Photograph probably c. 1930. (Unilever Collections,
Unilever Art, Archives and Records Management,
Port Sunlight)

introduced (Lever was a Freemason), with an organ also planned for the central hall (somewhat following the example of that in the Kelvingrove Art Gallery in Glasgow): all illustrating that Lever envisaged this as being more than just an art gallery. The central space around which the planning revolves is H-shaped, its main width governed by Leighton's huge Daphnephoria, which is displayed on one of the end walls, and which Lever had acquired in the McCulloch sale in 1913. It became a particular favourite of his and on his death in 1925 he lay in state under the picture. The hall was originally finished with black painted walls, perhaps an odd choice to modern taste, but black was enjoying some popularity at the time: Lutyens, for example, used it in his own drawing rooms; Vanessa Bell in her Charleston bedroom; and its use crops up again later in one of the Bauhaus professors' houses at Dessau. The Lady Lever was clearly in the forefront of fashion in this respect.

Beyond the central hall at either end of the building are the two Sculpture Halls, both domed rotundas, where at Lever's suggestion the encircling columns were coupled in pairs, with excellent effect. Smaller rooms were planned around these three main spaces: eastern rooms were planned for the intended Library, and on the west, the room given over to Masonic use. With a domed Reception Hall, the W arrangements are grander internally than the others. All interiors are plastered, except for the vestibules, where Hopton Wood stone of excellent ashlar finish gives a feeling of exceptional quality and solidity; inner rooflights of the domes are patterns of coloured glass. The larger galleries have fine enriched classical doorcases; all were originally such, but when the building was tampered with in the 1960s, those in the smaller rooms were destroyed and the openings reduced in size. A large basement room (called the Banqueting Hall) is inexplicably of bogus Tudor teashop style, some of its dark 'oak' being painted concrete.

Characteristic of Lever's taste and concern for education were five 'period' rooms incorporated in the gallery, their range and style mirroring that of the eclectic rooms in his own houses, and intended to provide authentic settings for some of his collection of furniture. Three are panelled: the 'Tudor and Stuart', 'William and Mary' and 'Early Eighteenth Century' rooms (Fig. 64). All three were supplied by London dealers, two by the firm of Litchfield and Co. (who also supplied panelling for Lever's restoration of Hall i'th Wood, Bolton; to his Wirral residence, Thornton Manor, and to his London house, The Hill), and they were all adapted to suit the spaces of the gallery. An 'Adam' room was designed by the decorator and furniture historian Percy Macquoid shortly before Lever's death and executed by the fashionable decorators White Allom, who had undertaken work in such notable places as the Frick Collection, New York and Polesden Lacy in Surrey. Finally, there was a 'Napoleon Room', designed by the archi-

tects and loosely based on the decorative scheme in Empress Josephine's Boudoir at Malmaison. Lever himself was deeply involved in the display and arrangement of the collection, and concerned himself with the design and finishing of each room, visiting the building at least twenty-three times between February 1920 and December 1922, when the gallery was finally opened.

Refurbishment and sympathetic remodelling to extend and improve facilities for visitors has been undertaken in a number of phases: in 1987–89 by the firm of Edmund Kirby (whose founder designed three cottage blocks in the village), an internal staircase was introduced near the SW corner and at a lower level, with access provided by a new external ramp, new shop and display space formed – this last more recently converted into children's workshop facilities.[2] In 2008, a ramped access to the W entrance was created by Purcell enabling this to become the principal formal entry point to the gallery in place of the restricted S doorway, and subsequently the S end display rooms have been sensi-

Fig. 64 Lady Lever Art Gallery. The 'Early Eighteenth Century Room', with fittings of c. 1730 from a house at Chatham. (Unilever Collections, Unilever Art, Archives and Records Management, Port Sunlight)

tively restored, unpicking some misguided alterations which had been made in the 1960s.

The Lady Lever Art Gallery was opened officially by Princess Beatrice, youngest daughter of Queen Victoria, in 1922, and its contents remain the most munificent of all Lever's public benefactions. The gallery is a monument not only to his wife, but also to his love of beauty and to his fervent belief in the worthiness of art and its power for good upon the human mind and spirit.

On display in the Lady Lever Art Gallery are, first, the works of art which Lever transferred from his huge private holdings to the gallery on its completion in 1922, and, secondly, the collections, mainly paintings, which he purchased in the last years of his life specifically for inclusion in the gallery. A few works were acquired after his death by the gallery's trustees, and some important paintings, notably by Rubens, were sold around 1958–61. Like many northern industrialists in the late nineteenth century, Lever began collecting paintings by rather conservative contemporary artists in the 1890s. He had, however, a special interest in art derived from his expertise in advertising soap and he incorporated in these advertisements reproductions of contemporary paintings, having first purchased the originals for this purpose. His taste later became more eclectic to embrace eighteenth-century British art, particularly portraits, and Pre-Raphaelite paintings. He was one of the pioneer collectors of eighteenth-century British furniture and in this field the gallery's holdings are unequalled outside London. His enthusiasm for eighteenth-century English design can also be seen in the gallery's large and representative collection of Wedgwood pottery, which also includes many of the original wax models commissioned by Wedgwood for execution as low relief decoration. Lever's taste in seventeenth- and eighteenth-century Chinese ceramics was equally catholic, extending not only to porcelain but also to cloisonné and Canton enamels and to jades and hardstones; in these areas, the gallery's collections are exceptionally rich, with *famille verte*, *famille noire* and blue and white porcelain of great richness and variety. He was too conservative a collector to be interested in earlier Chinese wares, and this conservatism is also apparent in his notable collection of classical sculpture, of which he was probably the last major British private collector. Lever amassed a large proportion of his collection from other notable collectors – Thomas Hope for classical sculpture and Greek vases, Richard Bennett and Sir Trevor Lawrence for Chinese porcelain, Lord Tweedmouth for Wedgwood, George McCulloch for contemporary paintings, James Orrock for eighteenth-century pictures and furniture – and the Lady Lever Art Gallery is probably the best surviving example of late Victorian and Edwardian taste.[3]

Notes

1 Lady Lever Art Gallery Archives. Transcript of copy letter. Lever to Segar Owen,
   2 August 1913.
2 Details of the work were supplied by Mr A. M. Macdonald of Messrs Edmund Kirby.
3 Paragraph contributed by Edward Morris.

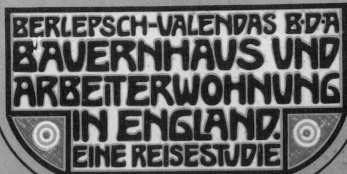

BERLEPSCH-VALENDAS B·D·A
BAUERNHAUS UND ARBEITERWOHNUNG IN ENGLAND.
EINE REISESTUDIE

ESZLINGEN a. N.
PAUL NEFF VERLAG
(MAX SCHREIBER)

7

Fame and Influence

Lever's flair for publicity made it unlikely that Port Sunlight would remain unknown, and from the very beginning it achieved fame. As early as 1890 an article appeared in the *Illustrated London News*, followed by another in 1898; the visit of W. E. Gladstone to open the Gladstone Hall in 1891 focused public attention on the village; its buildings were regularly illustrated in the architectural press, and the illustrated text of Lever's address of 1902 to the Architectural Association on *The Buildings Erected at Port Sunlight and Thornton Hough* passed through two editions. In 1909 appeared W. L. George's study of *Labour and Housing at Port Sunlight*, followed in 1916 by the profusely illustrated *Port Sunlight*, by T. Raffles Davison, editor of the *British Architect*, a friend of Lever's, and a noted architectural draughtsman.

References and acclaim are to be found in books and journals abroad as well as in Britain, not least in the work of Hermann Muthesius, whose writings were largely responsible for making the significance of English domestic architecture known on the continent. In *Das Englische Haus*, he wrote, 'If one wishes to obtain a quick and accurate appreciation of the achievement of contemporary English house-building, there is hardly a more comfortable means than by undertaking a journey to the factory village of Port Sunlight near Liverpool'.[1] Elsewhere, and more lyrically, he noted, 'Port Sunlight will always be honoured with the highest recognition. For it is here that the gates of a new world were first opened; in place of the dismal appearance of utilitarian buildings we were shown a new vision; in place of the misery associated with the barren rows of workers' terraces we find joyfulness and homeliness'.[2] Particularly noteworthy also were two other publications, one produced by an American architect from St Louis, E. W. Beeson, *Port Sunlight: The Model Village of England*, and the other written by a Swiss architect and artist, H. E. Berlepsch-Valendas, *Bauernhaus und Arbeiterwohnung in England*, which reported enthusiastically and at length on the development of the village (Fig. 65). Reproductions of Port Sunlight cottages were erected at the international exhibitions in Paris (1900), Glasgow (1901), and Brussels (1910). That at Paris, in the annexe to the exhibition at Vincennes, was visited by the French president, and the Brussels block was awarded the Grand Prix in the social and economic section. The Glasgow cottages were, after the exhibition, presented by Lever Brothers to the Glasgow Corporation, and may still be seen in Kelvingrove Park (Fig. 66).

Fig. 65 Hans Eduard Berlepsch-Valendas, *Bauernhaus und Arbeiterwohnung in England. Eine Reisestudie*, c. 1904. The cover of this study of Bournville and Port Sunlight shows a stylised drawing of Nos. 89–92 Greendale Road (William Owen, 1894), shown with eaves-level timber balustrade, now removed.

Fig. 66 Cottages erected at the Glasgow International Exhibition of 1901. These cottages were a copy of Nos. 2 and 4 Park Road, Port Sunlight and were built in Kelvingrove Park as part of the Lever Brothers' display. They were presented afterwards to the city where they still remain, seen here with Kelvingrove Art Gallery in the background.

Fig. 67 Lever Brothers' exhibition stand at the World's Fair in Chicago, 1893. The firm had received a Royal Warrant a year earlier and used this as an excuse for an elaborate stand supporting a huge model of Windsor Castle, made by the London specialist decorator and model-maker, Campbell Smith and Co. To accompany this, a booklet was published by Lever Brothers, which included descriptions of the stand itself as well as both the Castle and Port Sunlight – this last being a reprint of the article which had earlier appeared in the *Illustrated London News* in 1891. (Lever Brothers, *Windsor Castle at Chicago*, 1893)

Models of Port Sunlight at exhibitions and conferences also spread the word. Lever had quickly realised the potential of models on trade stands, beginning with his commissioning models of the factory at Warrington. These were made under the direction of William Owen in 1887, for exhibitions in Manchester, Newcastle and Liverpool, and all made by the firm of Hammonds. More spectacularly, following granting of the Royal Warrant in 1892, was the construction of a vast model of Windsor Castle which formed the canopy over the Lever Brothers' stand at the 1893 World's Fair in Chicago. This was made by the celebrated

WINDSOR CASTLE AT CHICAGO.

Fig. 68 George V and Queen Mary with Lever and the Earl and Countess of Derby seen inside the Hulme Hall with the model of Port Sunlight used in the ceremony of laying the foundation stone of the Lady Lever Art Gallery, 25 March 1914. Note the press button in the position of the future Gallery. (Leverhulme Family Archive)

decorator Campbell Smith of London and was accompanied by a booklet produced by Lever Brothers on the history of both the castle and the village (Fig. 67).[3]

Several models of Port Sunlight itself were built of which only one now remains and which is on show in the Museum. Its origins are obscure although it is known to have existed in the 1960s when it was on display in the entrance lobby to the company offices and was reportedly being brought up to date by Brian Kendrick. It has been periodically updated, recording demolitions, new building and the modernisation programme and now shows the village as it was in 1984. Other models known to have been built include one exhibited at the 1900 Paris Exhibition and one made of plaster by the architects Shepheard & Bower in 1914. Another model was made by Bassett Lowke, and two more have associations with Lever's patronage of the Liverpool University School of Architecture and Civic Design Department. No doubt it was one of these which was used in the Hulme Hall as part of the remote foundation stone ceremony for the art gallery, the press button being sited on the model in the position of the future gallery itself (Fig. 68); but others were used at town planning conferences – one on display in the Bluecoat School, Liverpool in March, 1914, for example.

A further model, made by the Liverpool sculptor Tyson Smith as one of his earliest commissions, was displayed at Patrick Geddes's Civic Exhibition in Dublin, in 1914, where numerous miniature buildings were stolen by local children, much to Lever's amusement.[4] Whether or not this model was repaired there and then is unclear, but, if it was not abandoned, it would have lasted little longer, as it would otherwise have been lost in the Indian Ocean, with the rest of the exhibition, on its way to an intended tour of India, but whose voyage out on the SS *Clan Grant* was abruptly terminated off the Maldives by the famous German First World War raider, the *Emden*.

The village provided inspiration for a musical comedy. *The Sunshine Girl*, by Paul Rubens and Arthur Wimperis, and produced by George Edwardes and J. E. Malone at the Gaiety Theatre in 1912, was set in Port Sunshine, the model village of a soap factory, and quotations from Port Sunlight architecture were included in one of the backdrops.

Visitors to Port Sunlight were, to say the least, encouraged. The first souvenir brochure for the factory and village appeared as early as 1891, and, although the first was the largest and most sumptuous, it was followed by a long series of others, revised and kept up to date as the village grew and changed. In 1909 alone no less than 54,000 visitors saw over the factory, and it was largely to cater for sightseers that the Bridge Inn was built. Gladstone was but the first of many distinguished guests, who included Asquith and Lloyd George, as well as the Bulgarian Prime Minister, Field Marshall Sir George White, and the Crown Prince of Siam. Albert, King of the Belgians, went to look at the village in about 1903, while travelling incognito before succeeding to the throne. Above all, there was the visit of King George V and Queen Mary in 1914. The royal guests toured the factory and the village, and the king laid the foundation stone of the Lady Lever Art Gallery. The opening ceremony, in 1922, was performed by Princess Beatrice. The Prince of Wales (later King Edward VIII) paid a visit in 1931 and in 1934 the Duke of York (later George VI) opened the group of cottages which bear his name, while more recently the Queen visited in 1957 and again in connection with the 1988 centenary celebrations.

Of greatest significance were the countless visits of labour delegations, industrialists, government officials and architects, of many nations. An early follower of the example set at Port Sunlight was Bournville, which had been founded near Birmingham in 1879 by George Cadbury, in connection with his cocoa and chocolate manufacturing business. Only in 1894, though, did extensive development begin, and, with W. Alexander Harvey as architect, Bournville proceeded on the low-density lines and with the concern for the overall environment which Lever had already established. In contrast to Port Sunlight, residence at Bournville was not initially confined to company employees, and a broader social spectrum was embraced. Moreover, the village was economically self-supporting, and its simple and informal style of architecture virtually established a norm. Between them, the examples of Port Sunlight and Bournville were of fundamental importance in furthering the garden city and garden suburb movement, in which Lever took a direct interest, and also in establishing the standards and styles of much of the best housing of the first half of the twentieth century. The architects and planners Barry Parker and (Sir) Raymond Unwin were key figures in this evolution, and the influence of Port Sunlight (including the development of the superblock plan) is apparent in Unwin's own work.

The third industrial 'garden' village to be established was New Earswick, near York, begun in 1902, with Unwin as architect. Like Bournville, it is not tied to the factory, and responsibility for it was placed in the hands of the autonomous Joseph Rowntree Village Trust, founded in 1904. By then, the concept of the self-sufficient and independent garden city, as expounded by Ebenezer Howard, was achieving reality, with the building of Letchworth. It was begun following the formation of the First Garden City Company Ltd in 1903, and the adoption of a plan by Parker & Unwin. Although he was to resign over policies of land availability, Lever was initially a director of the company. In 1902 the Garden City Association (formed to pursue the implementation of Howard's ideas) had met in Liverpool under Lever's presidency. Howard was in attendance, and the conference members visited Port Sunlight. As C. B. Purdom noted, in referring to Port Sunlight and Bournville, 'the immense value of these villages as actual object lessons on a small scale of the practicability and commercial advantages of the proposals put forward by Mr Howard was incalculable'.[5] Inspiration for the Housing and Town Planning Act of 1910 also owed much to them.

In 1910 a major and widely reported international town planning conference, organised by the Royal Institute of British Architects, included Port Sunlight among its options of places to be visited, with notes in the conference handbook contributed by (Sir) Patrick Abercrombie. It was, moreover, represented in the exhibition, organised by Unwin and held at the Royal Academy, which accompanied the conference. A plan, photographs of streets, and drawings of Ernest Prestwich's planning proposals were shown, chosen by Unwin himself. Among *beaux arts* planning schemes which may have benefited from contemporary publicity of Prestwich's scheme the Lutyens' plan for New Delhi and the Baron Empain's plans for Heliopolis in Cairo are but two.[6]

The eighth meeting of the International Housing Conference in 1907 (meeting in Britain for the first time) viewed Port Sunlight, and especially significant were visits of the French and the German Garden City Associations. This last included amongst its members Georg Metzendorf, architect of the Krupp model housing, as well as a young Mies van der Rohe.[7] Georges Benoît Lévy (Secretary of the French Association) and Bernhard Kampffmeyer (Chairman of the German Association) in their respective studies *La Cité Jardin* (1904) and *Aus Englischen Gartenstadten* (1910) were as enthusiastic about Port Sunlight as was Muthesius. Benoît Lévy had, in 1903, been sponsored by the Musée Sociale to make a close study of Port Sunlight and Bournville, and the English garden city and garden suburb movement did indeed inspire emulation on the continent, not least in architectural work by Muthesius himself.

Garden suburbs, owing much both visually and socially to the example of Bedford Park, differed from Letchworth not only in size but in being only social and not commercial entities. Most ambitious was the celebrated Hampstead Garden Suburb, of which Lever became a trustee, founded at the instigation of (Dame) Henrietta Barnett, and begun in 1906 to a plan by Parker & Unwin. Port Sunlight featured in its literature, and was illustrated by Dame Henrietta in lectures. The same tradition of cottage-style homes in spacious, healthy and pleasing surroundings was continued not only in the second garden city at Welwyn (from 1920), but in the best of the inter-war municipal housing estates, and it left its mark upon the post-1945 new towns.

Abercrombie, in his notes for the 1910 Town Planning Conference, wrote of Port Sunlight as being 'one of the earliest of the self-contained "garden villages", which has exercised an enormous amount of influence on English and foreign planning, and … as a clear example of picturesque arrangement dictated by natural necessities'.[8]

Some of this influence emanated from Lever's own addresses at conferences and speeches on world tours. But from the very beginning he realised that although Port Sunlight offered a vision for workers' housing and set standards to which others might aspire, it could not be regarded as offering a financial model. As early as 1898, in a speech in Birkenhead (and reiterated in his 1902 address to the Architectural Association), Lever noted that the only ways of achieving this commercially would be to have access to cheaper land and to build less-expensive houses. Part of the solution then he felt was to limit the number of houses that could be built on a given area to twelve houses to the acre, which would have a depressing effect on the value of land, but he also urged that councils should be active in purchasing peripheral suburban land on which could be built economical housing. This was a theme he returned to on a number of occasions, such as at the Conference of Municipal Authorities meeting in Sheffield in 1905; the 1906 Housing Conference, also in Sheffield; and his address to the Garden Cities Association in 1906.[9] In 1912, he put theory into practice by offering Birkenhead the Storeton estate, which he had purchased and begun to develop.[10]

The other side of the coin was building houses more economically. He urged 'less elaboration in architectural effects' at the International Housing Conference held in Port Sunlight in 1907 and suggested that 'a few sprays of ivy and a greensward in front of a house, a shrub here and there, and the plainest and most economical cottage, architecturally, becomes more beautiful than a more costly and elaborate one'.[11] It was a view promoted by many others in the reaction to Victorian excesses – Maurice B. Adams, architect of two blocks in the village in 1898, remarked that 'Cottage beauty has nothing in common with ostentation'.[12] This reaction can perhaps be seen at its best in Port Sunlight village in the block erected to the designs of Simpson and Holden at 30–38 Primrose Hill, of 1899 (Fig. 84), which relies as much on simple massing and proportion as architectural decoration – here restricted to a small, attractive, bas relief flower frieze, but it can also be seen in the unadorned blocks of cottages erected on the Woodhead and Bromborough Estates from around 1916, where, unlike in Port Sunlight proper, standard designs of houses were the norm (Fig. 27).

But, alternative, more economical building materials might also be explored, as he had urged in his 1902 Architectural Association speech: Lever had initially criticised Edison who had 'made a surprising proposal for about the lowest form of building – something about moulds in which cement had to be squirted'.[13] But by 1917 he had clearly mellowed and was promoting the idea of houses made from moulded panels cast in concrete, though it is not known whether he ever used this approach in any of his own housing schemes.[14] Elsewhere, in Lewis and Harris, perhaps prompted by Clough Williams Ellis's book, *Cottage Building in Cob, Pise, Chalk and Cob*, then just recently published in 1919, Lever experimented with cob pise construction and offered financial support and professional instructors to help islanders construct self-build houses with the use of standardised components.[15] He had been a patron of the Cheap Cottage Exhibition held in Letchworth in 1905, a popular demonstration of economical, partly experimental, house building, with houses being built for £150 or less, and the variety of construction methods being demonstrated, including concrete panel construction, would not have been wasted on him. Similarly, he was also on the organising committee of the Yorkshire and North Midlands Model Cottage Exhibition, which in 1907 built a group of model houses at Wincobank in Sheffield. However, in Port Sunlight proper, he resolutely stuck to traditional building methods, with generally some ornamentation despite the cost – cottages to standard plans being expected to be built for £330 each in 1901, with the larger Parlour houses £550.

Underpinning all this was perhaps a sense that Lever ultimately felt Port Sunlight had not completely fulfilled its early promise. Andrew Knox, a director of Unilever who knew Lever well, recorded that in the end Lever had felt that socially a mistake had been made owing to the stresses which develop when people work and live together and, as careers developed, staff tended to leave the village for reasons partly of social status, resulting in a less-diverse population than might otherwise have been expected.[16] Lever himself referred to home ownership being 'the badge of respectability' in a speech delivered in Sydney in 1914,[17] and actively looked at alternative ways of providing for this. In a movement beginning with Ealing Tenants Ltd., of 1901, many local schemes were launched under the auspices of Co-Partnership Tenants Ltd. Lever gave encouragement to a project in Warrington, and assisted plans for the formation of a tenants' company to acquire and develop part of the Bromborough Port Estate near Port Sunlight. At Port Sunlight he was able to purchase the nearby Edgeworth estate where he offered sites for individuals to build their own houses to approved designs, the first house being occupied in 1924, exemplifying his theory that provision of 'free land' for house building could be economic policy.

On a completely different level, Lever also promoted several speculative residential developments. He planned several estates connected to his network of elm avenues laid out in central Wirral from 1911, in one of which no less a person than Professor Charles Reilly made enquiries regarding a plot, but the main development was limited to an area at the northern end of the main avenue. At Lymm in Cheshire, acquisition of salt-bearing land arising from industrial rivalry with Brunner Mond left Lever with ownership of a sizable estate after settlement of the dispute, part of which Lever planned to develop as a high-quality residential development, employing W. & S. Owen in 1912 to provide plans for a layout with avenues and a bridge over the lake, but the development stalled. More successful was the scheme at Moor Park, Hertfordshire, in the outer parts of 'Metroland', where in 1919 Lever acquired the estate comprising the outstanding country house by Leoni, which he converted into a country club with a top-quality golf course, and developed a speculative estate alongside, planned by Mawson.

But whatever the merits or outcomes of these other schemes, it is Port Sunlight which has continued to spark interest and debate and to act as a major attraction in its own right.

In particular, the village has been able to appeal to each new generation: Josephine Reynolds writing in the *Architects' Journal* in 1948, felt that the village could still inspire as an example of a highly successful 'neighbourhood unit'. Twenty years later, albeit with some criticism, Nicholas Taylor included it in his examination of the pedigree of the modern house in his influential book *The Village in the City*, which argued against tall blocks and comprehensive redevelopment. Later still, Prince Charles, in his book *A Vision of Britain*, referred to Lord Leverhulme's own vision in creating the 'remarkable village of Port Sunlight'. Other commentators have similarly approached the village in their different ways: George Orwell commented favourably in 1936 on its 'excellent houses at fairly low rents', though considering it to be like publicly owned property in being 'burdened by restrictions',[18] while the populist travel writer Bill Bryson, writing in *Notes from a Small Island*, described it as 'worth every sodden step. Port Sunlight was lovely, a proper little garden community'.[19] Perhaps Theo Crosby described it better than any other when he wrote of it as 'a place we can learn from', and, with justifiable hyperbole, described it as '[the] first and only good housing estate in England'.[20]

There have of course always been critics of Port Sunlight; in more recent years, writers such as Roy Strong[21] have considered Port Sunlight and the garden city movement as being progenitors of suburban sprawl. But Lever was reacting to the problems of his day, and while it can be debated whether he would suggest low-density Port Sunlight as an exact model for mass housing now, many of its key features not surprisingly remain as valid today as in Lever's time: human scale and variety, provision of community and cultural facilities, eco-friendly layout and landscaping, opportunities to grow one's own food, ease of access to work, a mix of secure private and unthreatening public spaces etc. The garden city ideal, as exemplified and indeed partly initiated by Port Sunlight, remains an enduring and potent vision, with the government currently (2019) advocating building fourteen 'garden towns or cities', an approach likely to be increasingly endorsed in this post-Grenfell Tower age, when much of the thinking behind Port Sunlight seems likely to continue to influence housing policy well into the future.

Notes

1 H. Muthesius, *Das Englische Haus*, Berlin, 1904–1905, vol. I, p. 199. Translation by Mr Alan Johnson.
2 Quoted by Nicholas Bullock and James Read in *The Movement for Housing Reform in Germany and France*, 1985, p. 145.
3 Lever Bros, *Windsor Castle at Chicago*, 1893. Information from Peter M. Miller.
4 Philip Mairet, *Pioneer of Sociology: The Life and Letters of Patrick Geddes*, 1957, p. 150.
5 C. B. Purdom, *The Garden City: A Study in the Development of a Modern Town*, 1913, p. 25.
6 Robert Grant Irving, *Indian Summer: Lutyens, Baker, and Imperial Delhi*, 1981, p. 87 and ed John Rodenbeck, *Cairo*, 1992, p. 217.
7 Richard Pommer and Christian F. Otto, *Weissenhof 1927 and the Modern Movement in Architecture*, 1991.
8 Royal Institute of British Architects, Town Planning Conference 1910, *Members' Handbook*, p. 102.
9 *Garden Cities and Town Planning*, 1906, p. 68.
10 *Town Planning Review*, vol. 3, no. 4 (January 1913), pp. 223–24.
11 Lever speech in Port Sunlight, 8 August 1907, reprinted in Lord Leverhulme, *The Six Hour Day*, 1918, p. 182.
12 M. B. Adams, *Modern Cottage Architecture*, 1904, p. 13.
13 *RIBA Journal* (12 June 1909), p. 558.
14 Lever speech at Carlisle, 5 November 1917, reprinted in Lord Leverhulme, *The Six Hour Day*, 1918, p. 147.
15 Letter from Lever to Munro, 21 July 1920, Stornoway Town Council Town Clerk's Office files.
16 Andrew M. Knox, *Coming Clean*, 1976, pp. 9–11.
17 Robert Freestone, *Model Communities: The Garden City Movement in Australia*, 1989, p. 66 onwards.
18 George Orwell, *The Road to Wigan Pier Diary*, 1936; Penguin edition, 1970, p. 215.
19 Bill Bryson, *Notes from a Small Island*, 1995, p. 243.
20 Theo Crosby, 'The First and Only Good Housing Estate in England', *Journal of the Royal Institute of British Architects*, 3rd ser., vol. 83, 1978, p. 289.
21 Roy Strong, *The Spirit of Britain: a Narrative History of the Arts*, 1999, pp. 630–31.

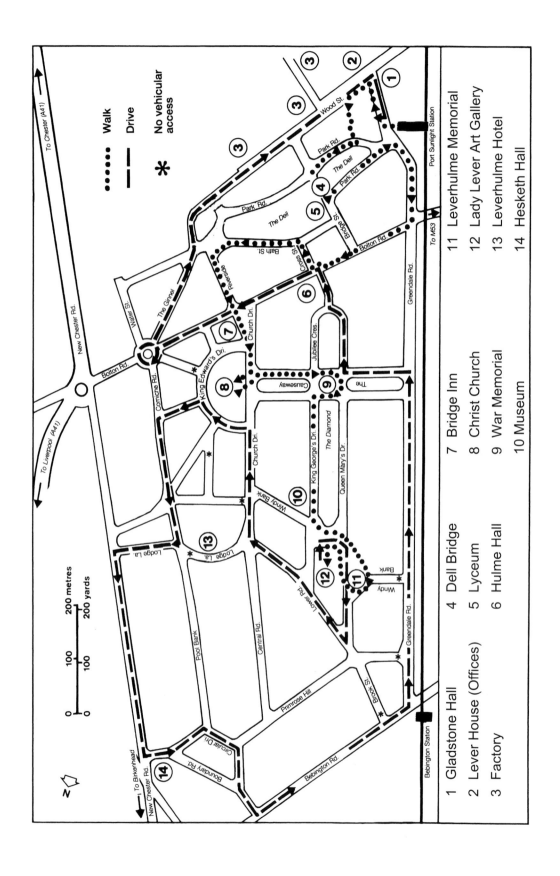

Key

•••••• Walk

▬ ▬ ▬ Drive

* No vehicular access

1 Gladstone Hall
2 Lever House (Offices)
3 Factory
4 Dell Bridge
5 Lyceum
6 Hulme Hall
7 Bridge Inn
8 Christ Church
9 War Memorial
10 Museum
11 Leverhulme Memorial
12 Lady Lever Art Gallery
13 Leverhulme Hotel
14 Hesketh Hall

Tours of the Village

Two routes are suggested: a walk supplemented by a drive; both being shown on the plan on p. 84. In these tours, L indicates left and R indicates right. Points of the compass are conventionally denoted: N, S, E, W. Note that most plans in this *Guide* are orientated with north to the left.

Walk: Port Sunlight Station to Lady Lever Art Gallery
Intended for visitors with limited time; includes the most important features and buildings.

PORT SUNLIGHT STATION. The station opened as a private halt in 1914, when the railway line was the mainline route into Birkenhead, as against the present electrified suburban Merseyrail. It was first used on the occasion of the official visit of King George V and Queen Mary to the village in order to lay the foundation stone for the Lady Lever Art Gallery, and it became a public station only in 1927. Today the visitor enters the village through the boarded station entrance hall, built originally in 1910 as the concert hall part of an Annex to the adjoining Lever Club but converted for railway passenger use 1919. Leaving this, and ahead is one of the noted views of the village: the vista from the top end of THE DELL, the first inlet to be drained and landscaped and the former inlet which forms the landscaped heart of the oldest part of the village, with, in the distance, the entrance front of the Lyceum. R into Greendale Road and past Nos. 89–92, a handsome block by William Owen, of 1894, a stylised image of which appeared on the cover of Hans Eduard Berlepsch-Valendas's study of Port Sunlight and Bournville, published in 1904. The former GIRLS' HOSTEL by Maxwell and Tuke lies next, now a bank and offices, including offices on the first floor of the Port Sunlight Village Trust. Gabled front, typical of the vernacular revivalism of the village's early days in its half-timber and bright red brick; three different framing patterns for the four gables, all in the midlands/north-west England tradition. Also a pargeted frieze containing figurative work as well as strapwork patterns. The building bears a plaque commemorating the award to the village of the 1993 Prix d'honneur, Entente Florale Europe. Wrought iron gates at either end of the building.

Opposite (but not its original site) is SILVER WEDDING FOUNTAIN (William Owen, 1899). Granite former drinking fountain, commemorating Mr and Mrs Lever's twenty-fifth wedding anniversary. Behind the bowling green, R to L:

Fig. 69 Interior of the factory in 1897. (Historic England Archives)

Fig. 70 Lever House (office building). Entrance Hall. By Owen, 1895–96, altered by Lomax Simpson, 1913–14. The stairs belong to Lomax Simpson's remodelling and their position is probably where Lever's glass-sided office had hitherto been; Royal Arms in mosaic floor (Lever Brothers having been appointed soapmakers to Queen Victoria, 1892). Photograph early twentieth century. Later, to commemorate Port Sunlight's 1938 Jubilee, busts of both the Lever brothers were placed on the newel pedestals of the stairs. (Unilever Collections, Unilever Art, Archives and Records Management, Port Sunlight)

Fig. 71 Factory Offices, East Wing (William Owen), seen in 1897. (Historic England Archives)

LEVER CLUB (a men's social club). Earliest part, originally called The Pavilion (Grayson & Ould, 1896) was built in connection with bowling green; it is the block nearest the railway. Half-timbered and formerly with a cupola; prominent extension (1968) is a not altogether successful attempt at sympathetic half-timber.

A HOUSE with half-timbered gable is the ENTRANCE LODGE which William Owen is known to have built, 1889, and which, with the accompanying stables (Gavin Hunter has shown) was first erected south of Wood Street but had to be taken down to permit expansion of the factory. Its design was used as the basis for the cottage erected at the Paris Exhibition.

Gladstone Theatre, originally GLADSTONE HALL (Owen, 1891, Fig. 39). The village's first public building. Simple and economical; large window areas combined with unostentatious cladding of tile-hanging (quite rare in the village though a common architectural feature of the period) and half-timber; copper Art Nouveau commemorative plaque by H. Bloomfield Bare, an architect/craftsman who had a studio in the village; later alterations by J. Lomax Simpson included addition of a two-storeyed porch housing a cinema projection room and backstage facilities. Front landscaping has been changed several times but now includes an accessibility ramp.

Fig. 72 Factory Offices (William Owen), seen in 1897 and possibly Lever's own office at that time given the personal nature of the pictures on the wall. View out onto the clerks' office in the distance. (Historic England Archives)

Beyond Gladstone Theatre is the FACTORY (see also pp. 93, 94). Visible is the office building (LEVER HOUSE), its stone entrance front in ornate free classical (Owen, 1895–96, Figs 70–72) and a more utilitarian higher block added in brick by Lomax Simpson, 1913–14, housing at the front a dignified panelled board room.

Walk towards factory: in front of 100 Greendale Road on left is a tree planted by the Queen in 1988 as part of the centenary celebrations. L into Wood Street. Many of the roads are clearly named after Lever's own personal connections – Bolton Road is the most obvious example, but others include here Wood Street, after the street in Bolton where he was born; Park Road, perhaps after Park Street, Bolton where Lever bought his first house; Windy Bank, the old name for Bridge Street, Bolton, at the bottom of which his father's business maintained a warehouse and where the Lever family lived briefly between house moves;[1] and The Wiend, a later group of houses immediately outside the village proper, perhaps after the narrow street of the same name in Wigan not far from the Lever family warehouse, though this is a general north-country word for passageway, like Ginnel, a name also used for a group of houses in the village. Others are named after local topography and planning features, such as Boundary Road, but some, less immediately apparent, are those with local village connections, such as Winser Street, after the first works manager and, formerly (now a footpath), Owen Street, after the first architect.

Fig. 73 Fire Engine Station. Probably built as stables, mid- or late 1890s; converted to fire station (for horse-drawn engines), 1906. Photograph, with motorised brigade, 1927. (*Port Sunlight News*, vol. 5, 6 July 1927, p. 201)

Fig. 74 Nos. 2 and 4, Park Road (Owen, 1892). A copy of this block was later erected at the 1901 Glasgow Exhibition; it remains in the city's Kelvingrove Park. To left, Nos. 6–12 Park Road (Owen, 1894). (Colin Jackson)

From Wood Street turn immediately L again for FIRE STATION (Fig. 73) or, as it more correctly proclaims, Fire Engine Station. Origin obscure, but probably late 1890s;[2] in use as stables 1902 and became Fire Station 1906. A charming building: two wings at an angle; timber used for minor elements only, but predominates in character over brick and tile. As may be seen by venturing behind, building is fitted into the otherwise useless space created by one of the first superblock enclosures (cf. Fig. 11). Two other contemporary and all subsequent such areas were large enough to contain allotments. Beyond Fire Station emerge into PARK ROAD, beside Nos. 2–4 (Owen, 1892, Fig. 74). The block which was reproduced at the 1901 Glasgow Exhibition: two houses but an irregular asymmetrical composition; Port Sunlight picturesque vernacular at its most fully developed and sumptuously enjoyable; pargetted gable, heavily enriched timberwork (bargeboards, bressumer, brackets) and patterned framing. Down Park Road. On R, more houses by Owen; on L THE DELL. Landscaped fragment of top end of S branch channel, and the most readily recognisable survival of the tidal creeks. Pedestrian DELL BRIDGE (Douglas & Fordham, 1894, Fig. 9). The surface of the soft sandstone shows the effect of having been grit-blasted some years ago, but care was taken to protect the quality of Neo-Jacobean ornament, and ball finials were reinstated correctly. Grouping with the bridge is the LYCEUM (Douglas & Fordham, 1894–96, Fig. 9). Originally The Schools and also used for Sunday services, now in use as a club, cafe and offices. Free Jacobean style and equally free grouping; in scale with surroundings but has dignity and distinction appropriate to education and worship; varying elements subtly suggest the intended dual function (windows with Gothic touches but gables looking more domestic; corner bell turret). Diapered brick.

Cross bridge and up opposite side of Park Road. All houses on R are 1892. Nos. 19–23 (Douglas & Fordham, Figs 75, 76) are bigger than the standard cottages. The group is terminated by BRIDGE COTTAGE (No. 23). One of the largest houses in the village and seemingly designed with a view to Lever's future use. It was used by him intermittently, particularly during 1893–97, partly while Thornton Manor was being extensively rebuilt. Lever carried out minor alterations and retained the property until around 1901, after which it was occupied by various key tenants, including a schoolmaster at the Park Road Schools, the curator of the Hulme Hall Art Gallery and later an industrial chemist.[3] Following use as the Vicarage from 1982 until 2014, it has been bought back by Port Sunlight Village Trust and currently (2019) is used as a 'Community Hub'. Although in the same group as 19–21, it has its own completely different character. Facing material of cut limestone fragments (not flint) as used by Douglas & Fordham earlier at the Castle Hotel, Conwy (1885) and later at Nos. 49–55 Wood Street (1895). End elevation with awkward projecting chimney arises from ground floor internal altera-

Fig. 75 Nos. 19–23 Park Road (Douglas & Fordham, 1892). Bridge Cottage (23) in foreground. (Unilever Collections, Unilever Art, Archives and Records Management, Port Sunlight)

Fig. 76 No. 21 Park Road. Timber details. (Unilever Collections, Unilever Art, Archives and Records Management, Port Sunlight)

tions made by Lever himself before 1901. Plaque commemorating Lever's connection unveiled in 1952. Nos. 19–21 have half-timber above a brick ground storey; beautifully detailed woodwork (carved bargeboards and bressumers, with an inscription on that of 19, and small oriel windows with traceried lights); all three houses have decorative leaded glazing. Twisted brick chimneys are a standard pattern: built up of purpose-made bricks, they were designed by Douglas & Fordham for mass production by a Ruabon manufacturer. Nos. 9–17 (Owen, Figs 10, 39) is simpler, but the topmost block, Nos. 1–7 (Owen, Figs. 37–39), has two gorgeously pargetted gables; letters 'LBL' for Lever Brothers Ltd (a limited company was formed 1890); the four cottages are mirror images in plan, but differ in elevation either side of the gables. Park Road shows Port Sunlight exuberance fully fledged.

Less elaborate, but equally pleasing, is the half-timbered corner TEA ROOM (Grayson & Ould, 1891, Fig. 45), built originally as a general store and then used as a POST OFFICE, but in its present use since 2007. R into GREENDALE ROAD to see that it forms part of a larger block (all same architects and date) and terminates a row of tile-hung cottages (Nos. 83–88). These are plain compared with Park Road's

Fig. 77 Cross Street (Grayson & Ould, 1896). (Unilever Collections, Unilever Art, Archives and Records Management, Port Sunlight)

Fig. 78 Bath Street (Talbot, 1895–97). Drawing by T. Raffles Davison (*Academy Architecture*, 1899, vol. 16, pp. 14–15)

opulence, but even more economical were the earliest cottages built (Owen, 1889–90); among them are three blocks comprising Nos. 74–78, with tile-hanging and white-painted oriels. R into BOLTON ROAD where Nos. 2–12 (modernised and remodelled as Nos. 8–12), on R, are simpler still, without tile-hanging. No. 1 (Owen 1889) on opposite corner of Greendale Road, was formerly two houses, Nos. 1 and 3 Bolton Road, where in No. 3 the architect J. J. Talbot lived during 1896–97. No. 15 (Grayson & Ould, 1891) is one of the larger houses, virtually a small villa, and the home of Edward Wainwright, who had been Lever Brothers' first soap-boiler at the Warrington factory. On R of Bolton Road, a post-war semi-detached pair, occupying site of Nos. 14–18, the very first cottages built, but which were destroyed in an air raid. Next, an open space on Bridge Street corner, is site of shops – Employees' Provident Stores and Collegium (Douglas & Fordham, 1894), destroyed in air raid. From here can be seen Nos. 8–14 BRIDGE STREET, a post-war reconstruction with frontage a close, but not exact, reproduction of the original (Grayson & Ould, 1894).

Continue down Bolton Road. On L, Nos. 17–21 (Owen, 1890). A block of three larger houses, occupied early last century by the minister, doctor and schoolmaster and probably built for professional men initially; the first attempt at any elaboration of treatment and materials, with some half-timber, though pebbledash predominates; now flats. A sensitive conversion in 2006 by Paddock Johnson Associates removed a later added unsightly rear staircase. No. 21 was the home of Thomas Ralph Nickson, who acted as clerk of works for the erection of many of the early village buildings. Further on L, HULME HALL (W. & S. Owen, 1900–1901, Fig. 47). Began life as women's dining hall; single-storeyed; Neo-Jacobean, of brick and stone, generously windowed; surmounted by large half-timbered gables with some enrichment. Hardly ostentatious by Port Sunlight standards, but the interior was designed with a view to quality, and it is the building which Lever considered excessively extravagant. Later in use as the art gallery, then as a public hall, it provided the setting for two of the Beatles' early concerts, commemorated by a plaque by one of the entrance doors. On 20 Bolton Road, opposite, a tablet records impromptu visit by George V and Queen Mary, 1914. This cottage is end return of Nos. 1–9 CROSS STREET (Grayson & Ould, 1896, Fig. 77). Walling of small biscuit-coloured bricks sets off red diapering, purpose-made bricks and ornamental terracotta; French and Germanic elements, particularly French Late Gothic dormers; blank panelling; slight recession between shallow cross-wings. View across lawns and bowling green, formerly tennis lawn to Lyceum; brick twisted chimneys belong to a Douglas & Fordham school extension of 1898. At this side of the building a rare survival: one of the hanging signs suspended from a post, such as were once a feature of the village. L into BATH STREET. The Dell, on R, is site of the vanished Auditorium, the site of its former proscenium close to the plaque unveiled by the third Viscount Leverhulme in 1988 in commemoration of the village centenary. Nos. 3–33 (J. J. Talbot, 1895–97, Fig. 78). A splendid red brick group, strong, solid and rather Dutch-looking; rhythm of gables – some large and freely shaped – and graceful white dormers; effect weakened by under-scaled turret; some chimney-stacks are panelled blocks, some clustered shafts. Comprising eighteen dwellings in all, this is the largest block in Port Sunlight and completed the earliest stage of the village. The first use of a boldly set-back plan, here defining a green. (On the grass a pedestal carries a curious sphinx sundial, age and origin unknown, restored to commemorate the millennium). A courtyard enclosure is implied by two long ranges and one short, the form being determined by the curving boundary of The Dell. Plan is ingeniously staggered round several corners, lining up with the Cross Street block and, round to the L, with 1–8 RIVERSIDE (Grayson & Ould, 1896, Fig. 18). With this latter is seen a material not hitherto encountered, cement render – much used in the village from the mid-1890s, in association with brick, for simple work. Here, though, in a lavish front, with features including tile-hanging and heart patterns of other materials set in the plaster.

Open space beyond this point is the ghost of the main channel; even after the land was levelled, housing intended for the site by Prestwich never materialised. Some development had been stimulated on the further bank by the Victoria Bridge (Owen, 1897) which extended Bolton Road to link up with New Chester Road and what little had by then been built on the E perimeter. Shorn of its parapets and buried under Bolton Road, the eponymous Victoria Bridge still exists near the BRIDGE INN (Grayson & Ould, 1900, Figs 18–20, 49). Beside the hotel is a depression (now planted) retained to light the kitchen when the channel was filled in. On this elevation is a bold grouping of chimney-stack, bay window and half-timbered gable. Nowhere else does half-timber appear, but dark-stained (not black) oak is much used. With colour-washed roughcast this provides the softer character and feeling for texture of materials typical of the early twentieth century; may be contrasted with the harder feel and crisp detail of Hulme Hall. Though Victorian in date, Bridge Inn is more Edwardian in character; has much in common with garden city movement, not only in appearance, but in the ideal of health, purity and sobriety with which it was conceived. Large overhanging gables; U-plan with verandahs of cross-wings cosily enclosing a forecourt; the verandah glazing is a later insertion, and the porch a tactful addition by Lomax Simpson. No original internal character remains; removal of simple and appropriate genuine Victorian fittings continued in 1980s, giving way to heavy pseudo-Victorianism; the fine dark-panelled dining room is altered beyond recognition. Large rear extension by the then Estates Department of Unilever Merseyside Ltd, 1964, which does not quite possess the expansive spirit of Merry England hospitality which the 1900 building so happily exudes.

So to Church Drive and CHRIST CHURCH (W. & S. Owen, 1902–1904, Figs 19, 20, 53–55). Of Helsby sandstone, ashlared outside and in. Lever Brothers' own Building Department were main contractors; stone carving by J. J. Millson. Like Lever's other ecclesiastical buildings, the form is fully church-like, its Congregational origins belied by long chancel with choirstalls and a reredos; clerestoried nave with narrow passage aisles, double N transepts;[4] tower in angle of S transept and chancel. Conventionalised Late Gothic forms and details with strong horizontal emphasis externally. Squat proportions consistent with twentieth-century late phase of Gothic Revival also help to integrate the building into its village setting, as does the domestic character of the stone-flagged roof. Fresh and lively departures from strict historical precedent include conventionalised tracery and the inward curving buttresses which break through the aisle roofs. The mouldings, also, belong unmistakably to c. 1900, rather than to the late Perpendicular of 400 years previously, which is the basic stylistic inspiration. Interior less successful, though undeniably impressive; Gothic still done with enthusiasm and roof carpentry over the chancel especially rewarding. Indiscriminately rich fittings (made by Hatch & Sons of Lancaster), with the organ by Henry Willis & Sons, perhaps the most famous organ builder of the twentieth century. Several stained glass windows by Heaton, Butler and Bayne in conventional late nineteenth-century style, very different from their earlier work; all are Lever family memorials; E window (1909); N transept (1912), W window (1914) and S transept (1931), more striking and colourful than the others. In contrast are the two brightly coloured and expressionistic windows by the Hungarian Ervin Bossányi (1950), one in either aisle; the commissions being the result of Charles Holden commending him to Lomax Simpson.[5] Worth a glance for its figure of St George, carved by H. Tyson Smith, is the Boys' Brigade Memorial (1931) at the W end.

Inscription of foundation stone (1902) in W wall faces inwards to the church, the idea of the external Lever burial place having by then been conceived. LADY LEVER MEMORIAL (so-called 'narthex' but more strictly a loggia) built against external W wall 1913–14 to a design which had been made by W. & S. Owen, 1905 (Fig. 56). Follows Perpendicular precedent more closely than does the church proper. Highly decorated – pinnacles, niches, etc., and rib-vaulted internally. Bronze recumbent effigy of Lady Lever (Sir W. Goscombe John, 1915) on black marble tomb-chest plinth; companion effigy of Viscount Leverhulme (Goscombe John, 1926) on a similar plinth; seated children originally at the base of the first plinth were repositioned centrally against the two; separate memorial bust of second Viscount Leverhulme (1949, by Sir Charles Wheeler, now lost); enclosing grilles by the Owen firm, 1935; nearby in churchyard are two attractive Barnish family memorials (a family with Lever associations) probably by Lomax Simpson. Note exceedingly huge and heavy outer door of church; timber-framed lychgate (W. & S. Owen, 1905).

On leaving church, notice on opposite corner Nos. 1–5 CHURCH DRIVE with Nos. 5–7 THE CAUSEWAY (W. & S. Owen, 1901). Frontage to The Causeway is set at an angle, being intended as the beginning of a line to skirt the then still existing middle branch channel.

Fig. 79 NE junction of The Causeway and The Diamond. Nos. 1–4 King George's Drive with Nos. 8–12 The Causeway (Lomax Simpson, 1911–13). Photograph probably c. 1914. Note modestly scaled gas street lamp. Cf. Fig. 24. (Unilever Collections, Unilever Art, Archives and Records Management, Port Sunlight)

WAR MEMORIAL (Sir W. Goscombe John, 1916–21, Figs. 33, 57) where The Causeway and The Diamond intersect. Its being 'a rare example of a war memorial which is genuinely moving and which avoids sentimentality' is an observation quoted more than once, but originating from one of the present writers. Granite structure adorned with bronze sculpture. Central runic cross encircled with a wonderful life-like group in the round (so much so that limbs and drapery overflow the plinth). The idea is 'defence of the home'. Soldiers guard women and children and a wounded comrade whom a nurse is about to tend; a seated woman cradles a group of infants, and a frightened little girl stands, guarded by her equally frightened but brave and defiant younger brother; a Boy Scout stands with the soldiers. Against the parapet of a surrounding enclosure are large panels in high relief, breaking forward into the round, and representing the Anti-Aircraft (NW), Naval (SW, Fig. 57), and Military (SE) Services and the Red Cross (NE). Bas-reliefs on parapet piers depict children offering wreaths for the fallen.

THE DIAMOND in its present form was laid out in 1910 as the central boulevard of the replanned village (Fig. 24); the name dates from when branch channels cut diagonally across at either end. Entirely built by J. Lomax Simpson, 1911–13 (Fig. 25), with end blocks returning to face The Causeway. Early-twentieth-century use of gentler materials and exploitation of texture seen in rustic brick, colour-washed roughcast

Fig. 80 Part of block comprising Nos. 23–30 Queen Mary's Drive, The Diamond (Lomax Simpson, 1911–13). (Unilever Collections, Unilever Art, Archives and Records Management, Port Sunlight).

Fig. 81 The Diamond: Queen Mary's Drive looking towards the Lady Lever Art Gallery. Nos. 31–46 Queen Mary's Drive to left (J. Lomax Simpson, 1913). (Colin Jackson)

and woodwork less sharply defined than in earlier work; the effect would have been softer still when the oak was (as originally) left in its natural state rather than blackened (as now). In contrast may be seen, looking towards the railway, the end RH block – Nos. 18–34 The Causeway with Nos. 44–48 Greendale Road (Talbot, 1902) displaying the more insistent materials of earlier years.

Roofs of The Diamond include some which are of North Country stone flags; built into brickwork are fragments of random-looking masonry, implying, in the manner of George Devey, an imaginary centuries-long evolution (Fig. 79). KING GEORGE'S DRIVE forms RH (E) side of The Diamond and QUEEN MARY'S DRIVE the L (Fig. 81). Take the former. Until the new trees reach maturity both sides will remain visible from each other. The challenging problem of reconciling grand formal planning with Port Sunlight's vernacular cottage architecture was solved with consummate skill. The centres of both sides of The Diamond are symmetrically recessed, opposite each other, thus imposing a cross-axis and implying a quadrangle, and both recessed ranges have three large gables. Though both sides are thus similar in general massing, within this discipline enormous variation occurs; both facing ranges differ from each other and neither is fully symmetrical in itself. Picturesque elaboration is as great as that which marks any of the earlier buildings of the village, with resourceful but unobtrusive differences of grouping, detail and materials; rustic brick, roughcast, stone, half-timber (including brick nogging), weather-boarding, etc. The far end of King George's Drive undergoes mutation from the character of domestic to public building, being terminated by the MUSEUM, originally the Girls' Club opened as a heritage centre by the Village Trust in 2006 (Lomax Simpson, 1913, along with the rest of The Diamond, Fig. 81); indicative of Lomax Simpson's masterly planning of tight sites – here an acute angle, the centre point of the Club Room is also the point of intersection of the lines of the converging rear walls of the adjoining cottages; transition made by an attached cottage block but which is separate from the main group and which, with a hipped roof, has a subtly more formal, classical feel. The club itself, with a pair of tall and dignified Jacobean stone bay windows, emphasised an important corner, opposite which the Lady Lever Art Gallery was about to be built; an unexpected touch of half-timber lurks round the far corner.

FOUNTAIN, at end of The Diamond, near art gallery. Lively sculpture by Sir Charles Wheeler, 1949. 'Sea Piece', exhibited at the Royal Academy in 1949 and gifted to the village by the Trustees of the Gallery to commemorate the birth of Lady Lever in 1850. To the L (W) of art gallery, the LEVERHULME MEMORIAL, unveiled 1930 (Figs 30, 31). The designer was Lomax Simpson, the sculptor (Sir) William Reid Dick – the same association as at Unilever House, London, of c. 1929–31 and reflecting Lomax Simpson's unease with Goscombe John and what he felt was over-elaboration and complexity of the earlier War Memorial design. An obelisk and its square fluted base are of polished granite and have something of the 'streamlined' styling of the period. Consistent in character is the crowning figure of Inspiration, which was shown outside Lutyens' British Pavilion at the 1930 Antwerp Exhibition; in contrast to its Expressionism is a group of more realistic figures at ground level, representing Industry, Art, Education and Charity – ably composed and modelled but rather over-heavy in its symbolism and lacking the vitality of Goscombe John's war memorial.

The setting of the Leverhulme Memorial is worthy of note, being the vista which Lomax Simpson opened up on the W axis of the art gallery, c. 1924–26. This brilliant piece of urban surgery involved curtailing rows of cottages in Greendale Road and Windy Bank. The latter range (Grayson & Ould, 1902) had been built alongside the N branch channel, aligned SE. Of it there remains Nos. 6–11 Windy Bank, with No. 6 refaced where truncated. To balance the fragment and create a crescent effect, a new half-timbered block was built (numbered 5 Windy Bank with 17–22 Queen Mary's Drive). This repays careful study. Not symmetrical, though at first glance seemingly so. End groups of gables differ, in framing patterns as well as general massing; chimneys do not correspond; the more one looks, the more do subtle and entertaining variations and delightfully imaginative touches present themselves.

Note tiny gabled windows looking inwards along the main roof. Also built as part of the scheme, 1926, are two pairs nearer the railway, almost facing each other and linked with their neighbours by screen walls containing shell niches: Nos. 2–4 Windy Bank (with two gables), a reconstruction of the block by Grayson and Ould which was dismantled to permit construction of the new roadway; and Nos. 1–3 (hipped and more formally conceived, Fig. 30). For related work in Greendale Road see p. 105.

Now, the great LADY LEVER ART GALLERY itself (William & Segar Owen, 1913–22). The introverted mass is satisfactorily related to its setting, and, writing to Lever, Segar Owen described how their desired objective might be achieved. He referred to 'keeping a simple building with the entrances as the outstanding features', and to 'long lines giving this large building a low dignified appearance [which] would, I think, harmonise with the Village, but at the same time stand out quite apart'[6] (Figs 25, 58).

The classical language is spoken clearly and grammatically and a number of subtleties may be noted. The four entrances (all fluted Greek Ionic – the order used throughout the building) comprise three different designs, only the N and S porticoes being identical; all four entrance features project from the main block; those at the N and S are linked by quadrant re-entrants which read as the main corners of the building. These not only prevent harsh and abrupt edges, but form elements in the taut and concentrated end elevations – the S end has to exist as an independent entity closing The Diamond (Figs 25, 58). In contrast, portals on the long and otherwise featureless side elevations are strengthened by wider spacing and richer treatment of windows (Figs 31, 62). Included here possibly at Lever's own wish, these windows are emphasised by apron panels below, heavy framing and, particularly, by trophies above, depicting the arts. E and W entrances differ not only in plan, but in application of enrichment to the classical members (both pairs of windows vary in this respect also). Crispness of moulding and erudition of detail everywhere contribute to a classical *tour de force* such as seldom fell to the lot of an English architect to realise.

Large urns at S entrance were placed subsequent to completion of the building. Enclosure of protective railings (even here a regrettable necessity) of 1987 by Bruce Hyslop Ltd in association with the Property Department of the then National Museums and Galleries on Merseyside.

Skyline with central mass, and at either end a shallow dome, expresses the internal plan; core is a high Main Hall of elongated H-plan lying between two Sculpture Halls, both domed rotundas; smaller rooms are arranged round and between these main elements.

Drive: Lady Lever Art Gallery to Station

A longer route, including features not seen in the walk, and a selection of further noteworthy cottages.

Art gallery marks site of W end of N branch channel, the S and N edges of which are perpetuated by the curving lines of Windy Bank and Lower Road respectively.

Clockwise round gallery; in its NW corner, the marble *L'OPPRIME PRENANT CONSCIENCE DE SA FORCE* (by the French sculptor A. G. Guilloux, 1913), originally placed in the grounds of Thornton Manor, then later still to the east of the gallery,[7] into LOWER ROAD. On L, Nos. 15–27. Built 1906, before the gallery, by Professor (Sir) Charles H. Reilly, who induced Lever to take interest in the Liverpool School of Architecture and later to found the Chair of Civic Design. Shallow crescent of Mediterranean feel; continuous verandah with recognisably Reillyesque details and round-headed dormers with scrolly side volutes. Rather incongruous in Port Sunlight, despite Reilly's usual scholarly classicism being muted. Verandah supports surprisingly in timber and not cast iron as would be expected. Nos. 29–33 and 35–49 (two ranges both by Lomax Simpson, 1906, Fig. 82); set back forming a green, originally to enclose established beech trees; some tile-hanging. Next, Nos. 51–59 with 66–72 CENTRAL ROAD (Lomax Simpson, 1906, Fig. 83). A half-timbered corner block planned at an acute angle with a large gable as a focal point; though there are fewer tricks than in later work, the architect here also plays a teasing game of 'spot the asymmetry' (e.g. placing of chimneys). On the opposite corner, MANOR LODGE (Lomax Simpson, 1939–40), built as a nurses' home for the nearby Cottage Hospital, converted to flats by Paddock Johnson Associates, 2004.

R into CHURCH DRIVE, passing on L grounds of LEVERHULME HOTEL (Grayson & Ould, 1905–1907, Fig. 51). Former Cottage Hospital, entered from Lodge Lane, converted (2008) to hotel use. Due to pebbledash, not immediately recognisable as Neo-Georgian, a style more usually associated with brick; sash windows (rare in the village). Original appearance changed by additions on S (W. & S. Owen) and N (Lomax Simpson). Two alternative schemes for laying out the grounds were made by Mawson, 1906. On R is open space marking position of N branch channel; view across to Nos. 23–24 WINDY BANK (Grayson & Ould, 1907, Fig. 40). Intended as Belgian style, as part of the plan (abandoned soon after) to build cottages representing countries where Lever Brothers had factories; the bricks were imported from Belgium. Large corner turret with conical roof; small stepped gable; a larger gable has straight sides but with steps implied by carefully graded brick; other brickwork of equally excellent workmanship, e.g. arch of doorway curved in two planes. On L, CHURCH DRIVE SCHOOL (Grayson & Ould, 1902–1903). Loose

Fig. 82 Nos. 29–33, 35–49, 51–59 Lower Road (Lomax Simpson, 1906), planned around existing trees. Drawing by Sydney R. Jones, a well-known illustrator and topographical writer, friend of both Lever and James Lomax Simpson. (British Architectural Library/RIBA)

and free grouping of diverse elements, mainly from 'Queen Anne' revival – the classical counterpart of Port Sunlight's 'Old English' and here used with equal irregularity of composition. The building stood near edge of the main channel, hence deep depression at rear, with playground remaining below present surrounding ground level. This, and an oriel window, may be seen by driving first L into KING EDWARD'S DRIVE and then round further into stump of a blocked road belonging to the now partly closed system, laid out 1910, radiating from the church. Back to and continue round King Edward's Drive, then L, with a view of the long panorama of CORNICHE ROAD, which ran alongside the main channel. L into Corniche Road. On R, No. 53 was the home of Jonathan George Davies, one of the early photographers of the village; Nos. 31–35 (one of the surprisingly few Port Sunlight buildings by Jonathan Simpson, father of J. Lomax Simpson, 1899). A rather awkward flat-topped dormer, but also lovely floral Art Nouveau decoration in shallow pargetting. Charles Holden (later to achieve distinction with his London Transport and London University commissions) was working for Simpson at the time.[8] Is it fanciful to discern here the hand of an outstanding but still immature architect? Nos. 17–23 (1897–99). Indeed, there is little indication of the genius which had for some years already been apparent in the earliest of (Sir) Edwin Lutyens' Surrey houses and which had placed him in the forefront of domestic architects. Yet this is by no means a negligible work; porches and their roofs and the asymmetry of the tile-hung portions are worth analysing; Venetian windows give special character, but there is nothing of the mastery of materials which was his forte and which Lomax Simpson later displayed to such good advantage in The Diamond. At the corner of POOL BANK and LODGE LANE, PHILIP LEVERHULME LODGE (Paddock Johnson Architects, 2000). A block of ten flats with use of traditional materials and details in sympathy with the Port Sunlight character.

R into LODGE LANE. On L, Nos. 12–20 with 69–75 POOL BANK (Grayson & Ould, 1898). Rather hard, both in its brick and in its 'Queen Anne' classicism, yet still rooted in Port Sunlight vernacular in eschewing sash windows and strict symmetry. Symmetrical portions to Pool Bank (with pair of bay windows) and Lodge Lane (with pediments) but informality is introduced with other blocks (including the linking portion of what is a staggered corner plan). Turn L into NEW CHESTER ROAD, leaving behind the exclusive tranquillity of the village.[9] On the corner Nos. 212–16 (W. & S. Owen, 1898). Another corner plan, here effectively generating unusually complicated massing; also exceptional is the range of motifs in the decorative brickwork set in rendering (the original now replaced with pebbledash); some tile-hanging; porch with a corner post (recognisable as an Owen feature); very exceptional for Port

Fig. 83 Nos. 51–59 Lower Road with 66–72 Central Road (Lomax Simpson, 1906). (Unilever Collections, Unilever Art, Archives and Records Management, Port Sunlight)

Sunlight, and possessing particular character, in rising in part direct from the pavement.

Continue along New Chester Road. Of cottages by well-known London architects, built in the late 1890s, the most successful are those of Ernest George & Yeates. By them, on L, Nos. 178–90, 1897. E-plan with a forecourt recessed between cross-wings; roughcast, a pargetted gable and leaded glazing. Re-enter village proper at next on L for BOUNDARY ROAD and CIRCULAR DRIVE, but first see HESKETH HALL (former Technical Institute) on opposite corner. After a long period in use as the Port Sunlight branch of the Royal British Legion, it now houses fourteen apartments following a major reconstruction by Paddock Johnson Architects in 2014, which included removal of an unsightly rear escape stair and conservation of the impressive gable decorative reliefs. Begun 1902 by J. J. Talbot, the year of his death, extended 1904–1905 by Grayson & Ould. Pebbledashed entrance front with Venetian windows; only a modillion cornice gives any hint of the thrill in store round the corner in New Chester Road (Fig. 50). Ould's usage of seventeenth-century domestic elements at its most opulently spectacular: two pargetted gables, an oriel with arched middle light, a big half-octagonal bay and a frieze with richly pargetted panels; equally elaborate brackets carry one gable; background of the plaster relief featuring is now painted dark – no historical precedent for this, but it is stunningly successful. View of Nos. 3–47 Boundary Road (Grayson & Ould, 1905). The frequently used device of two ranges at right angles set back to form a triangular enclosure; informal, with effectively placed gables; the group was originally terminated by two shops at each end but only those at the south remain. Nos. 18–26 Circular Drive (Grayson & Ould, 1906). A generously scaled ogee cupola articulates the corner of this angled block and an arched porch nestles up against its lower stage. View L down PRIMROSE HILL. Of the straight roads in this N end of the village, this is the most attractive, with the character of cottage grouping enhanced by the gradient and with several blocks by 'Lever' architects. Of particular note is that by Jonathan Simpson, Nos. 30–38, one of the more progressive blocks in the village of the time in terms of massing and use of simple geometric forms, identifiable as the cottages on which Holden is known to have worked (Fig. 84).

L into BEBINGTON ROAD and out of the village environment again. On L, Nos. 57–65 (W. & S. Owen, 1899); steep roofed end pavilions and dormers with curved pediments. Nos. 67–79 (Ernest Newton, 1899). Not recognisable as his work, but a simply treated elevation with clever use of overlapping symmetry (well worth studying); screens of turned balusters at the porches. Across the road, i.e. outside the village, is the LIBERAL CLUB (J. J. Talbot, 1902–1903), almost certainly built by Lever.[10] Back in the village, Nos. 89–97 (Wilson & Talbot, 1897–99, Figs 35, 36). Some good touches (e.g. decorative panels incorporated with the main upper windows); overall impression is of steep hipped roofs, including dormers and larger half-hips, and of dark wood used for minor features.

L into GREENDALE ROAD – the long display facing the railway. On the corner, DUKE OF YORK COTTAGES (Lomax Simpson, 1933–34, Fig. 86), built as pensioners' houses. The block sinuously wraps round a service court; public face has varying materials (stone, plaster, brick, half-timber), but used for successive parts of the frontage, rather than blended in close harmony as at The Diamond; some symmetry; stone roofs. At the far corner of PRIMROSE HILL is work by Lomax Simpson, 1925 (Nos. 55–57 Primrose Hill and, planned diagonally on the corner, Nos. 3–6 Greendale Road). Dark rustic brick and of the neat, refined, underlyingly classical category, but still drawing on seventeenth-century domestic elements – timber mullions and leaded glazing, and, on the Greendale Road block, three shell door hoods. Nos. 6K–10 Greendale Road (Grayson & Ould, 1901) are the remainder of the block from which two cottages were removed in the course of cutting through a vista to the art gallery by Lomax Simpson, c. 1924–26 (see p. 32). So well was the side of No. 10 refaced, with a bay window added, that no-one could suspect that amputation had taken place. KENYON PEEL COTTAGES – Nos. 11–17 (J. J. Talbot, 1902, Fig. 41). A close copy, though reduced in scale, of the timber-framed Jacobean Kenyon Peel Hall, not far from Bolton (demolished 1957). Shallow E-plan front

Fig. 84 Nos. 30–38 Primrose Hill (Jonathan Simpson, 1899); perspective by Charles Holden, who is known to have worked on this block for Simpson. (*Building News*, 21 July 1899)

COTTAGES AT PORT SUNLIGHT.

with extruded corners; characteristic north-western patterned timber framing; patterned leaded glazing. Nos. 25–29 and 33–39 (both Ernest George & Yeates, 1901). Fresh and lively in an unassertive early-twentieth-century way; roughcast; massive Lutyens-like chimneys; Nos. 25–29 with three hips; the other has a long front, with unequal treatment of gables either end.

L into THE CAUSEWAY. On the far corner, Nos. 49–52 Greendale Road with 1–4 The Causeway (Grayson & Ould, 1901). The trouble with the dramatic spire-like roof which crowns the corner pavilion is that the lines of half-round ridge tiles cannot all continue unbroken – the feature is a good idea, but not fully resolved in terms of practical detailing. Before War Memorial, R into S end of Queen Mary's Drive. On L, view of JUBILEE CRESCENT (Lomax Simpson, 1938). Dating from the village's half-centenary, and the last set of cottages built. Brick, some tile-hanging and weather-boarding. An extended, picturesque group of two separate blocks, one of them wholly irregular, the other with elements of symmetry and subtle variations; lacks the joyful and imaginative zest of earlier work and is rather inadequately integrated in its broad open setting. Continue round by the formal layout which closes the vista of The Diamond (Lomax Simpson, 1933–34) and which includes BALUSTRADED TERRACE, GARDEN and ARCH. Memorial tablet to victims of the Hillsborough disaster of 1989 set within gardens. R by arch and L into BOLTON ROAD. Continue across site of main channel (which still remains as open space, though intended by Prestwich for housing) to roundabout (planned as a *rond point* for 'Village Cross'). Beside it Nos. 64–78 Bolton Road (W. & S. Owen, c. 1912). General character is Edwardian, with splayed wings a version of the 'butterfly' plan. Fourth exit from roundabout is THE GINNEL. Ranges on L comprise Nos. 1–35 (Lomax Simpson, 1914). They include two forming a triangular green; difficult to analyse, so great is the diversity of materials (brick, roughcast, some pargetting in smooth-plastered gables) and elements (Doric columns, oriel windows, casements with glazing bars); overall flavour is classical, despite informal layout. In its neat, clean-cut way, the group is as imaginative and satisfying as the slightly earlier housing in The Diamond. Behind on Wharf Street three-storey sheltered accommodation by Paddock Johnson Architects.

L across end of The Dell to POETS' CORNER. On R, site of the demolished SHAKESPEARE COTTAGES. Also on R, Nos. 2–8 with 50–52 Park Road (Grayson & Ould, 1894). Corner turret with square spire forms pivotal point for half-timbered front to Park Road and shorter return to Poets' Corner. Edward Ould's black-and-white expertise shows up the less convincing adjoining work at 38–48 Park Road (T. M. Lockwood, 1895). Rest of Poets' Corner elevation not fully resolved as a composition, but displays virtuoso use of brick and terra-

Fig. 85 Greendale Road, looking towards the factory with offices (Owen, 1895–96) and higher offices behind including board room (J. Lomax Simpson, 1913–14) with (on left) Nos. 89–92 Greendale Road (Owen, 1894) and the former Girls' Hostel, later Lever Library, and bank and Heritage Centre. (Colin Jackson)

Fig. 86 Duke of York Cottages (Lomax Simpson, 1933–34). Photographed during final stages of construction, probably 1934. (Unilever Collections, Unilever Art, Archives and Records Management, Port Sunlight)

cotta with quiet, neutral background of cement render; diaper patterning and, more particularly, windows integrated with blank panelling; terracotta used for pediments on doorways and cusped heads of panels and window lights.

R into WOOD STREET, one of the straight perimeter roads. Here the houses face the FACTORY, which, needless to say, has undergone numerous enlargements, rebuildings and other alterations since 1888. Early parts were almost entirely single-storeyed (planned thus by Lever for efficiency in what he termed 'concertina' planning, the enclosed open space permitting departments to expand and contract) and original frontages remain. All of Ruabon brick; neatly handled, but with no special features, and contrasting with the beauty of the village.

On R, Nos. 27–35 and 37–47 (Grayson & Ould, 1895). Flemish character; brown brick; large stepped gables with brick spiral finials; smaller curved gables built up in brick. Opposite these two blocks is the front of the original factory (Owen, 1888–89, Fig. 15). A four-storey part behind had a belvedere tower at the far L (SE) corner. A distinctive feature, this marked the spot where Mrs W. H. (later Lady) Lever cut the first sod inaugurating Port Sunlight. Sadly it was removed in 1970. Prominent landmarks seen from further afield in Wirral were tall factory chimneys, demolished in the 1950s. Next along Wood Street is the surviving front of an extension (also Owen) of 1893, with terracotta date inscription. Opposite this wall, a view R into BRIDGE STREET: on L, Nos. 16–22 (Owen, 1894, Fig. 87). A sturdy block with two differing half-timbered gables and ashlared (sandstone) masonry playing an important part; brick twisted chimneys, thinner than Douglas's standard pattern. On opposite side of Bridge Street, Nos. 1–9 (Douglas & Fordham, 1893–94). No stone dressings; brick and terracotta used exclusively – for walling, coping of curly Dutch gables, mullions, traceried spandrels, cusped heads of window lights; brick diapering; roofs of corner turrets are rather Germanic in profile.

Continue up Wood Street. On R, Nos. 17–23 (Douglas & Fordham, 1892). Patterned woodwork, particularly bargeboards; pargetted gables, with swirling, almost Art Nouveau designs, combined with comparatively staid strapwork. Next on L, LEVER HOUSE (W. Owen and W. & S. Owen, 1896 and 1909) with very long E and W office wings extending either side of the stone centrepiece seen earlier (see p. 88). Until done away with in alterations by Lomax Simpson, 1913–14, behind the entrance was the legendary Chairman's Office, from which Lever looked down through glazed walls at the long rows of clerical workers either side.

R into GREENDALE ROAD and return to PORT SUNLIGHT STATION.

Notes

1 A list of some of the names is given in *Port Sunlight News*, February 1954, pp. 40–41. This suggests Park Road may simply be named from its location overlooking the Dell.

2 Not to be confused with a separate fire station at the factory (Owen, 1895).

3 Information from the Village Trust and Gavin Hunter.

4 Compass points are given according to traditional liturgical orientation, assuming the chancel to be at the E end.

5 Jo Bossanyi and Sarah Brown, *Ervin Bossanyi: Vision, Art and Exile*, 2008, pp. 176–77.

6 Lady Lever Art Gallery Archives. Transcript of copy letter. Segar Owen to Lever, 23 August 1913.

7 Edward Morris and Mark Evans, *Lady Lever Art Gallery, Catalogue of Foreign Paintings, Drawings, Miniatures, Tapestries, Post-Classical Sculpture and Prints*, 1983, p. 121.

8 Information on Holden at Port Sunlight kindly communicated by Mr Eitan Karol. A panel of similar decoration occurs at Nos. 30–38 Primrose Hill.

9 The frontage of cottages to this main road extends for more than half a mile and includes many by the several architects most active at Port Sunlight in the 1890s, particularly Grayson & Ould. One of their terracotta French dormers of Cross Street (see p. 56) appears at Nos. 288–92 and a pair at Nos. 240–42 (all 1898). Also examples of the simple treatment of cement render relieved by brick chequer and diaper (mostly by Grayson & Ould and W. & S. Owen).

10 Mrs Kirkwood, the club secretary, confirms that ownership of the property was transferred from Lever to his son in 1909.

Fig. 87 Nos. 16–22 Bridge Street (William Owen, 1894) seen in 1897 with the factory in the background to the left. This is one of the blocks illustrated in *Englische Baukunst der Gegenwart* by Hermann Muthesius. (Historic England Archives)

Demolished Buildings

This list does not include the many cottages which were repaired or rebuilt in exact external facsimile after air-raid damage in the Second World War, nor the few cottages and houses already on the site when Lever arrived and which were demolished as the village expanded. These included, for example, a mission chapel, an alms house, various cottages and a large detached house, Pool Bank, home of a mayor of Birkenhead in the early 1890s. There was also a cement works on the quayside complete with lime kilns, but this was eventually demolished following acquisition by Lever Brothers for expansion of the factory site. The list relates to the village only. For some reference to the factory see p. 108.

NOS. 14–18 BOLTON ROAD (Fig. 7). By William Owen, 1889–90. The first cottages built at Port Sunlight. Asymmetrical block of three with tile-hanging. A version was built at the 1910 Brussels Exhibition. Carried an Art Nouveau commemorative tablet, almost certainly by H. Bloomfield Bare, an architect/craftsman whose workshop was in Windy Bank. Destroyed in an air raid and replaced by a semi-detached pair of different design.

NOS. 8–14 BRIDGE STREET. By Grayson & Ould, 1894. Destroyed in an air raid, and rebuilt with similar, but not exact, reproduction of original elevation.

EMPLOYEES' PROVIDENT STORES AND COLLEGIUM. Adjoined the above, on Bridge Street/Bolton Road corner. By Douglas & Fordham, 1894. Built for three co-operative shops, with Girls' Institute (later called Collegium) above. Destroyed in air raid.

SHAKESPEARE COTTAGES, Poets' Corner (Fig. 88). By Edmund Kirby, 1896. Two cottages built as a reproduction of Shakespeare's birthplace (that is, the nineteenth-century restored version of the house), and an idea perhaps suggested by the Poets' Corner in Old Manchester and Salford at the Manchester Royal Jubilee Exhibition of 1887. Unpopular because of its high cills and dark interiors, it was later used as the offices for the Building Department. Demolished 1938.

VICTORIA BRIDGE (Figs 18–20). By William Owen, 1897, its name commemorating the Diamond Jubilee. Built to carry Bolton Road across the widest channel. Not demolished, but buried when the final stage of filling in the channel took place, c. 1901–10. Still exists beneath the road, near Bridge Inn. Parapet was re-used on a railway bridge in New Chester Road and its inscribed stones reappeared at the 1984

Fig. 88 The now demolished Shakespeare Cottages (Edmund Kirby) photographed 1897. (Historic England Archives)

Liverpool International Garden Festival prior to being set up in their present location opposite the Bridge Inn.

FOUR COTTAGES IN GREENDALE ROAD, by Grayson & Ould, 1901 (between present Nos. 10 and 11 and attached to present Nos. 6K–10), and FOUR COTTAGES IN WINDY BANK, by Grayson & Ould, 1902 (continuing line of, and including two attached to, present Nos. 6–11 and a separate block of two). Demolished c. 1924 in opening up vista W of Art Gallery. Replaced by present Nos. 2–4 (a reconstruction of one of the earlier blocks) and 1–3 Windy Bank and by present No. 5 Windy Bank with Nos. 17–22 Queen Mary's Drive. Sides of present No. 10 Greendale Road and No. 6 Windy Bank were refaced. All by J. Lomax Simpson, completed 1926.

OPEN-AIR SWIMMING BATH (Fig. 89). On southern corner of The Causeway and Queen Mary's Drive. By William & Segar Owen, 1902. Dressing huts etc. were thatched. Closed 1971. Demolished 1975. Garden centre now occupies the site.

GYMNASIUM (Figs 17, 24). By William & Segar Owen, 1902. Originally built on present war memorial site. Was timber-framed and weather-boarded and thus not difficult to dismantle and re-erect when, in 1910 and in accordance with Prestwich's plan, it was moved to beside the swimming bath in S end of Queen Mary's Drive. Had housed Arts & Crafts and Home Arts Exhibition, 1904 (emanating from H. Bloomfield Bare's studio in the village). Later used as retail store by

Fig. 89 The open-air swimming pool looking north to the entrance, with the Gymnasium in its original position on the site later occupied by the War Memorial. Thatched changing rooms to the left. (W. & S. Owen, 1902). Swimming pool demolished 1975. (Unilever Collections, Unilever Art, Archives and Records Management, Port Sunlight)

AUDITORIUM.

Fig. 90 The Auditorium proscenium of 1902 in its original state before the seating area was encased within a vast hangar-like structure with temporary canvas and later permanent slate roof (Grayson and Ould, 1902–03). The bas reliefs were modelled by the Liverpool sculptor E. O. Griffith. Demolished 1937. (W. H. Lever, *The Buildings Erected at Port Sunlight and Thornton Hough*, 1st edn, 1902)

Unilever's Macfisheries company, and was Boys' Club before being demolished 1981–82.

AUDITORIUM, in E end of The Dell (Fig. 90). Began as proscenium stage (by Grayson & Ould, 1902–1905) and open-air theatre. Defeated by the weather. Was almost immediately given an iron frame for canvas covering. A solid enclosing structure built 1906, accommodating 3000 for large company and village gatherings; was also used as a skating rink. Unsightly and acoustics bad. Demolished 1937.

BANDSTAND (Figs 24, 25). By J. Lomax Simpson, 1905–1906. An open Ionic structure, first sited near N end of The Diamond. Moved to centre of The Diamond as part of the 1910 replanning. Demolished, probably 1932, when rose garden laid out and columns re-used in offices at Bromborough.

GREENDALE. A large detached house built for Percy J. Winser, the first works manager and later vice-chairman of the company, taken down to permit expansion of No. 4 Soapery in the factory and reconstructed as HEATHFIELD in Bebington, later demolished.[1]

SHELTERS TO BOUNDARY ROAD BOWLING GREEN. These Norfolk reed thatched shelters of 1932 were designed by Lomax Simpson in connection with use of the bowling green by the United Comrades Federation, later Royal British Legion, whose local association was based in the nearby Hesketh Hall following the First World War. The shelters were demolished early in the twenty-first century.

Note
1 Information from Gavin Hunter.

Notes on Architects, Sculptors and Craftsmen

The numerous architects who worked at Port Sunlight included many regularly employed by Lever elsewhere, and several firms and families stand out by reason of their influence on him, principally: the Simpson, Owen and Mawson families, Douglas & Fordham, Grayson & Ould and Professor Charles Reilly. Lists of selected architects and sculptors and craftsmen follow below.

Selected Architects

MAURICE BINGHAM ADAMS (1849–1933) was one of the group of London architects who undertook some limited work in the village around 1898. In Adams's case, two blocks, following which he is not known to have undertaken any further work for Lever. He was a gifted draughtsman and editor of *Building News* for over fifty years during which time it illustrated a number of Port Sunlight and Lever schemes. In London he undertook many of the libraries erected by the Cornish philanthropist J. Passmore Edwards (owner of *Building News*), generally in a jolly late-Victorian classical free style. The Passmore Edwards South London Art Gallery was designed by Adams and he designed a number of stylish houses and cottages. He was the author of several architectural books, including *Modern Cottage Architecture* (1904; 2nd edn 1912), which illustrated his two blocks at Port Sunlight. He lived in Bedford Park, London, a famous early garden suburb, and was the designer of some of its houses as well as being responsible there for the church hall and art school.

WILLIAM NASEBY ADAMS (c. 1887–1952) was a star pupil of Professor REILLY at Liverpool University and won the Lever prize for the design of a cottage block, which uniquely was erected as Nos. 5–13 Central Road, even though Adams was only aged eighteen at the time – a marvellous example of Lever being prepared to take risks and Reilly readily grasping the promotion opportunities offered to demonstrate the skills acquired at his School. After a period in practice in Liverpool, Adams joined Edwin LUTYENS in London and became his chief assistant on the Britannic House project. He later sat on the RIBA Council and various committees of the RIBA.

HENRY BLOOMFIELD BARE (c. 1848–1912) was responsible for one block of cottages in the village, 36–44 Central Road, of 1906. Like Reilly he is likely to have been an influence on Lever, helping to develop his interest in training in crafts and architecture. Perhaps best known for his contribution to the decorative detailing of the Philharmonic public house in Liverpool, Bloomfield Bare was a regular contributor to *The Studio*, and gave some lectures at the Royal College of Art. He was in practice as an architect in Liverpool, for a time with H. L. Beckwith, and practised briefly in Philadelphia in the early 1890s, where he was an active member of the city's Art Club. At Port Sunlight, he ran an arts and crafts studio at 14 Windy Bank and organised an important arts and crafts exhibition in the Gymnasium in 1903–1904. His daughter Ruth Bare became a designer at the Della Robbia Pottery in Birkenhead.

FREDERICK J. BARNISH (c. 1877–1950) was responsible for two blocks of cottages in the village and a third in connection with Garnett, Wright and Garnet of Warrington. The Barnish connection is an example of how Lever remained loyal to local friends, as Fred was the son of Lever's Wigan doctor, who had been in attendance at the birth of Lever's son. Fred was one of six children, of whom two, Crowdson William and Leonard, may be mentioned here: Crowdson joined Lever Brothers and became the director–manager of the Port Sunlight factory, and Leonard became a successful architect in Liverpool, joining George Hastwell Grayson in partnership. But it was Fred who undertook architectural work for Lever. After training at Liverpool University and working as an assistant to WILLIAM OWEN, he was from 1905 to 1909 chief assistant to Garnet, Wright and Garnet of Warrington, architects of cottages at the Warrington Garden Suburb from 1908 (whose commemorative stone was laid by Ebenezer Howard). He later established his own practice in Warrington, also giving occasional assistance to MAWSON and, after the war, assisting in Mawson's War Memorial Village in Lancaster. According to family tradition, Fred had a relaxed attitude to architectural practice and was out fishing when Lever once called in person at his office to inspect progress – an incident unlikely to have endeared him to the 'chief'.[1]

BRADSHAW & GASS was the leading practice in Bolton. Jonas James Bradshaw (1837–1912) and John Bradshaw Gass (1855–1939), his nephew, were joined in partnership by Arthur J. Hope (1875–1960) in 1903. The practice was responsible in Port Sunlight for the corner block of 2–14 Central Road and Primrose Hill of 1905, a block using their then favoured hard-pressed red brick and terracotta (seen, for example, in a number of their Wesleyan mission halls and mills of the north-west), but a design and with materials somewhat in contrast to the 'softer' appearance of the village cottage norm. Gass had worked earlier for

ERNEST GEORGE and became the main contact in the practice for Lever. They took part in Lever's Bolton School baths competition of 1903, acted as assessors for Lever in his Bolton School (main) buildings competition in 1918 and prepared town planning proposals for the centre of Bolton for Lever in 1924. In addition, there were designs for Lever's Mac Fisheries stores and, at the time of Lever's death in 1925, designs for a pavilion in Leverhulme Park, Bolton. Elsewhere, the firm achieved fame for their civic buildings built across Britain, won in competition, including town halls or libraries in Wimbledon, Stockport, Leith, Luton and Lewisham. The firm continues to practise successfully today.[2]

JOHN DOUGLAS (1830–1911) was a pre-eminent provincial architect, receiving national and some international recognition. He studied under E. G. Paley of Lancaster and practised in Chester from c. 1860 – as DOUGLAS & FORDHAM from c. 1884 and as DOUGLAS & MINSHULL from c. 1897. Douglas's prolific output was largely ecclesiastical and domestic, and included much for the first Duke of Westminster on the Eaton Estate. His work was highly praised by Muthesius in *Das Englische Haus*. It is of individual character, and marked by sure proportions, careful detailing and a fine sense of craftsmanship and feel for materials. Styles which influenced him included local timber-framing, and this would have especially appealed to Lever. Douglas was the oldest and at the time the most famous of Lever's favoured group, and the one most likely to have been uncompromising on matters of style. His general influence is apparent in much of Port Sunlight's architecture; the firm was also employed at Thornton Manor and Thornton Hough village, but nowhere does Douglas appear at his most imaginative and idiosyncratic. DANIEL PORTER FORDHAM (c. 1846–99) was probably the partner with whom Lever dealt, and the practice continued to be employed for only a short time after Fordham's premature retirement and death.

(SIR) ERNEST GEORGE (1839–1922) developed an extensive London-based practice, in partnership, first with Thomas Vaughan, then Harold Peto and latterly Alfred B. Yeates, known particularly for its domestic work of country houses and London town houses, including the famous group in Flemish style in London's Harrington Gardens. George was president of the RIBA, 1908–10 and at the 1909 annual dinner Lever spoke of having made 'Mr George's acquaintance many years ago' and said he had always been a great admirer of his work, for Mr George had done much to solve the difficult problem of making a home that was really a home beautiful in all its parts and yet convenient for modern usages, without degenerating into the appearance of town halls or public institutions such as workhouses, as was so often the case

… Mr Ernest George had realised the ideals of the English home – beautiful in every way – and they had reason to be proud that at Port Sunlight they had some beautiful examples of his work.[3] His houses at Port Sunlight are 178–90 New Chester Road, 25–29 Greendale Road and 33–39 Greendale Road; but despite praise for George at the RIBA he did not otherwise undertake any work for Lever.

THOMAS HAYTON MAWSON (1861–1933) was arguably the leading landscape architect of his time. He contributed little to Port Sunlight, but on the strength not only of Lever's gargantuan gardens, but of his eminence and the family friendship which developed, cannot be omitted from any list of the professional designers. From establishing his own nursery in the Lake District, Mawson undertook garden and public park design, gradually developing a world-wide practice in landscape and town planning, and contributing to the literature of both subjects. Clients included Andrew Carnegie and the Marquess of Bute, and from 1905, numerous projects were undertaken for Lever, whom he regarded as his most important patron. These included the gardens at Thornton Manor; Roynton Cottage, Rivington; the Hill, Hampstead; Lews Castle kitchen garden and the circular walled garden at Borve Lodge, Harris. Mawson tended to introduce formality and architectural treatment into landscaping, and in civic design shared Lever's admiration for grand and broad classicism, affined to the American City Beautiful movement. Lever's abortive planning proposals for Bolton were drawn up by him. Three of his sons joined the firm, which became T. H. MAWSON & SONS, with EDWARD PRENTICE MAWSON (1885–1954) taking a leading role after training at the Architectural Association School in London and the Ecole des Beaux-Arts in Paris. For a few years ROBERT ATKINSON (1883–1952) – later principal of the Architectural Association School – worked in association with the practice and was engaged on a number of Lever's commissions.

EDMUND KIRBY (1838–1920) established a leading practice based in Liverpool in 1867. For Lever, he was responsible only for the cottages in Port Sunlight at 49–53 Corniche Road and 40–50 Primrose Hill, as well as the, now demolished, block modelled on Shakespeare's birthplace at Poets' Corner, a block in which Lever took a keen personal interest. Kirby had been an assistant to Edward Welby Pugin and later John Douglas before establishing his own office which concentrated on religious and domestic buildings throughout the north-west. The firm still exists and has more recently been involved in work on the Lady Lever Art Gallery. There is an extensive archive of their work in the Liverpool Library Archives.

(SIR) EDWIN LANDSEER LUTYENS (1869–1944) studied architecture at the South Kensington Schools then spent a period in ERNEST GEORGE'S office before establishing his own practice concentrating initially on a range of Surrey house commissions gained mostly through connections through his wife and the garden designer Gertrude Jeckyll, for whom he designed Munstead Wood in 1896. His delightful early vernacular revival domestic work gave way to stylish classical designs and romantic interpretations, such as his repair and conversion of Lindisfarne Castle and the design of Castle Drogo. His famous commissions of the Whitehall Cenotaph and New Delhi were to come respectively in 1919–20 and 1912–31. Perhaps it was not surprising that Britain's most famous architect should be approached by Lever, but their brief relationship was distinctly cool, and apart from his block of cottages in Port Sunlight his other project for Lever, a hotel in Stornoway, progressed no further than a sketch plan. According to Lomax Simpson, who visited Lewis with Lutyens, when the Port Sunlight block was mentioned Lutyens said, 'Forget it!' And reports in the diary of his close friend Lady Sackville on Lutyens's return from the island are distinctly unsympathetic.[4] Lever achieved some success with Lutyens, however, by having a miniature bar of Sunlight soap carefully positioned in the basement scullery of the Queen Mary's Dolls' House, of 1924.

HUON ARTHUR MATEAR (1856–1945) was responsible for six blocks in the village. He became noted for robust and powerful designs – for example, Holy Trinity Church, Southport and the tramway power station in Stalybridge. His later designs in Port Sunlight show a tendency to a free style with, for example, curving parapets and angled dormers. He had been articled to the noted Liverpool architect James Francis Doyle and established his own practice there where, with F. W. Simon, he designed the Liverpool Cotton Exchange of 1906 – whose confident baroque frontage, demolished in 1967, is still much mourned. He is not known to have undertaken any other work for Lever outside Port Sunlight.

MAXWELL AND TUKE only designed one building for Lever – the Girls' Hostel on Greendale Road, Port Sunlight – but they were an important north-western practice responsible for major projects such as the laying out of St Anne's on Sea, from 1875; the design of Blackpool Tower, 1891–94; New Brighton Tower, 1896–1900; Southport Winter Gardens and many buildings in their home base of Bury. They were shortlisted in the major Admiralty and War Office building competition, London, of 1884, their plan for which was commended by *The Builder* as being 'one of the best'. There was other work by the firm abroad in Yokohama and in Ecuador.

EDWARD AUGUSTUS LYLE OULD (1852–1909) trained under Douglas, and for a short time practised independently in Chester. In 1886 he was taken into partnership by GEORGE ENOCH GRAYSON (c. 1834–1912), already a successful architect in Liverpool. In the firm of GRAYSON & OULD, the former was the businessman, the latter the artist. The practice, which included domestic, commercial and some ecclesiastical work, is best remembered for its half-timber revivalism. Ould was an expert on black-and-white architecture, to which he would have been introduced in Douglas's office. He was responsible for the text in a book of examples, and it was to him and Jonathan Simpson that Lever entrusted restoration of the partly timber-framed Hall-i'-th'-Wood at Bolton. His most famous work, however, is Wightwick Manor, Wolverhampton (now National Trust).

WILLIAM OWEN (1846–1910) was articled to John Lowe of Manchester and served as assistant to James Redford. In 1869 he opened his own office in Warrington, where he developed a successful practice, undertaking domestic, industrial and commercial buildings. An accomplished draughtsman, he received training from the Bolton artist Selim Rothwell. He carried out work at Lever Brothers' Warrington factory, became a close friend of Lever's, and in 1897 was made a director of the company. Owen was the first architect employed at Port Sunlight; his firm established the architectural idiom of the village, and was responsible for much of the early development. Two of his sons joined the practice: SEGAR OWEN, later Segar Segar-Owen (1874–1929), and GEOFFREY OWEN (1887–1965). Segar served with A. E. Street (son of G. E. Street) in London; trained at the Royal Academy Schools, and became his father's junior partner in 1898, the firm being styled William and Segar Owen. Geoffrey served with Dunn & Watson in London, before joining the family practice, and became a partner in 1912.[5]

THOMAS TALIESIN REES (1865–1943) was the architect of two blocks of cottages in the village and was locally based in Birkenhead, where he was responsible for one of the Liberal Club buildings gifted by Lever. Later he was based in Liverpool in partnership with Richard Holt and was responsible for a range of buildings, including hospital work and famously the moving and re-erection of the Edward Ould house, Bidston Court. Elsewhere, he was responsible for the Village Institute in Llanystumdwy, Caernarvonshire, largely paid for by Lloyd George.

Fig. 91 William Owen.

(SIR) CHARLES HERBERT REILLY (1871–1902) has been described as being more than any other individual 'responsible for determining the future shape of architectural education in Britain down to the present'.[6] He was responsible for only one block of cottages in the village, Nos. 15–27 Lower Road, of 1906, but owing to his influence on Lever's taste and patronage he must be mentioned here. On his appointment as Professor at the School of Architecture at Liverpool University in 1904, he had deliberately sought out Lever and persuaded him to take an active interest in its development. At the School, Reilly promulgated a grand American classical manner in both architecture and town planning and through his ambition and drive it became the dominant University School in Britain. This position was reinforced when he helped persuade Lever to found the Department of Civic Design at Liverpool in 1909, the first school of town planning in the country, and from 1910 to finance the *Town Planning Review*, its increasingly influential public voice.

JONATHAN SIMPSON (1850–1937) was Lever's closest friend; they first met at school. The two men shared similar tastes, and Simpson was also a connoisseur and collector. He was articled to a local surveyor, James Lomax, one of whose daughters he married, and he established his own architectural practice in Bolton, with an output of mainly, though not exclusively, domestic work. Stylistically it was eclectic, with marked Arts & Crafts and Queen Anne influences, and is seen at its best in his own house, Grey Gables, in the restoration of the cruck barns on Lever's Rivington estate and in several local public houses. For a while he employed as an assistant CHARLES HOLDEN (1875–1960), later to achieve fame for his work for London Transport and London University. Simpson designed only three cottage blocks at Port Sunlight, but would have had a powerful influence on Lever's taste.

JAMES LOMAX SIMPSON (1882–1977) was Jonathan Simpson's son and he later chose to add a hyphen to his name. Following school at Uppingham, he studied at Liverpool University and, on the recommendation of Lever (who was his godfather), became articled to Grayson & Ould. After setting up in practice in Liverpool in 1905, he worked in association with his father. He designed some forty cottages as well as the factory for Edward Peter Jones of the Mersey Iron Works

Fig. 92 A Simpson family photograph c. 1935/36, taken in the garden of Whinfold, Surrey, James Lomax Simpson's home from 1931 to 1940. Lomax Simpson is seated, with his father, the architect Jonathan Simpson, standing, his wife Mary Isabel (née Messenger), with their daughters, Josephine (1925–99), later to become a doctor, psychoanalyst and pioneer in group therapy, and Rosemary, later noted as an administrator, treasurer and patron of the Attingham Trust and professional flower decorator. (Rosemary Lomax-Simpson)

at Ellesmere Port, working alongside C. R. Ashbee, and worked on Jones's own house outside Chester. Other projects included several private houses, church extensions and a school, as well as commissions directly for Lever. He was appointed to take charge of the Architectural Department of Lever Brothers in 1910 and was made a director in 1917, but continued to undertake numerous personal Lever commissions, including work at Thornton Manor; The Hill, Hampstead; Roynton Cottage, Rivington; Lews Castle, Stornoway and model housing in Stornoway. A talented architect of great versatility, his work as company architect included overseas factories, work on buildings of Lever's associated companies and Unilever House itself. His assistant in private practice, and then later his deputy at Lever Brothers, was BERNARD TAIT AUSTIN (1873–1955), son of H. J. Austin of Paley and Austin fame. ERNEST PRESTWICH (1889–1977), winner of the 1910 Port Sunlight planning competition, worked for a while under Lomax Simpson at Lever Brothers before joining the practice of his father, J. C. Prestwich, in Leigh. He later worked in association with (Sir) Percy Thomas on a number of successful civic building competitions.[7]

JOHN JOSEPH TALBOT (1871–1902) was a native of Bolton, where his father was a schoolmaster. He practised only from the mid-1890s till his early death, but in that short time regularly exhibited at the Royal Academy. Besides designing many cottages for Port Sunlight (where he resided c. 1896–97) Talbot worked for Lever at Thornton Manor. Elsewhere, commissions included some large suburban houses, and his work is marked by stylishness, quality of materials, thoroughness and careful detail. Had he lived, Lever (who attended his funeral) would doubtless have continued to employ him. Talbot and WILLIAM GILMOUR WILSON (c. 1856–1943) were in partnership c. 1896–1900, practising in Liverpool and Bolton as WILSON & TALBOT. Wilson, who later developed a successful independent practice, had been an assistant to John Honeyman in Glasgow (the practice which Charles Rennie Mackintosh joined) and to William Owen in Warrington.[8] Later work included contributions to the idiosyncratic model seaside resort of Thorpeness in Suffolk.

Notes
1 Information from George Wilde and Sheila Lemoine.
2 Jane Linguard and Timothy Linguard, *Bradshaw, Gass and Hope*, 2007.
3 *RIBA Journal*, 12 June 1909, p. 558.
4 Letter, Nigel Nicholson to MHS, 22 August 1970.
5 Thanks are due for information and sustained assistance generously given by Mr Halsall Owen, son of Geoffrey.
6 Alan Powers, in Joseph Sharples (ed.), *Charles Reilly and the Liverpool School of Architecture, 1904–1933*, Catalogue to the exhibition at the Walker Art Gallery, Liverpool, 1996.

7 No acknowledgements relating to Port Sunlight are complete without mention of Mr Lomax Simpson, the last of Lever's architects to survive, and whose recollections of 'The Old Chief' and the building of the village were an invaluable source of knowledge.
8 J. Miles Broughton has conducted research concerning J. J. Talbot and W. G. Wilson.

Selected Artists, Sculptors and Craftsmen

RICHARD BECKETT had been the main contractor for extensions to Lever's confined Warrington factory buildings. He was John Douglas's brother-in-law, based in Hartford, Cheshire and was the contractor for many of the Eaton Estate buildings near Chester. At Port Sunlight, contracts which he gained included Ernest Newton's 67–79 Bebington Road, Jonathan Simpson's 30–38 Primrose Hill and Edmund Kirby's 40–50 Primrose Hill and 49–53 Corniche Road.

(SIR) WILLIAM REID DICK (1878–1961) was responsible with James Lomax Simpson for the Leverhulme Memorial of 1930. He was a notable sculptor of the 1930s who had trained at the Glasgow School of Art and, after war service, was responsible for work on a number of First World War Memorials including the lion crowning the Menin Gate in Ypres, of 1927. Noted for his Kitchener Memorial Chapel in St Paul's, of 1922–25, he worked with Lomax Simpson on the sculpture on Unilever House, London (1930–32) and was responsible for the two giant sculptures of horses – 'Controlled Energy' – which sit bookend-like at both ends of the curved frontage. He was later responsible for the stylish figure of George V erected in Old Palace Yard, Westminster, in 1947.[1]

(SIR) WILLIAM GOSCOMBE JOHN (1860–1952) was responsible for the two figures of Lever and his wife in the narthex to Christ Church and the village war memorial, one of his most important commissions. He was born in Cardiff, and after training at the Royal Academy and a year in Paris he became a leading exponent of the New Sculpture movement and undertook a series of commissions for public sculptures and monuments, such as the figures of Edward VII and Queen Alexandra outside the entrance to the Victoria and Albert Museum; the King's Liverpool Regiment memorial, 1905; the expressionistic Engine Room Heroes memorial, Liverpool, 1916; the figure of Edward VII on horseback for Liverpool, 1916 and David Lloyd George, Caernarvon, 1921. He was knighted in 1911. His daughter Muriel married Luke V. Fildes, the first company secretary of Lever Brothers and son of Lever's friend, the artist Luke Fildes.

JOHN JARVIS MILLSON was a leading Manchester architectural sculptor with a wide spread of projects, including work at All Saints, Stockport, Pownall Hall, Wilmslow, Bury Art Gallery and Lichfield Cathedral. At Port Sunlight he is known to have undertaken the stone carving on the front of the company offices of 1895, then external decorative carving at Christchurch in 1902–1904, the Lady Lever memorial, 1913–14 and then, still later, the Lady Lever Art Gallery, 1914–22 (this last shared with Earp, Hobbs & Miller), all for W. & S. Owen.[2]

ROBERT NEILL (1817–1899) & SONS was the main contractor for the 1888 factory. The firm was said to be one of the largest in the country at the time and, based in Manchester, was responsible for many major contracts throughout the north-west, including: the building of Todmorden Town Hall, 1870–71; the Atkinson Art Gallery, Southport, 1876; the building of Manchester Central Station, 1875–80; the rebuilding of Liverpool Exchange Station, 1886; Bolton Station, 1898, and the building of Manchester's Great Northern Warehouse, opened in 1898. The firm was also the contractor for the reconstruction of Old Manchester and Salford in the 1887 Manchester Exhibition. Neill was Mayor of Manchester, 1866–1867 and became High Sheriff of Rutlandshire.[3]

Fig. 93 Robert Neill. The contractor for the first factory (W. Burnett Tracy and W. T. Pike, *Manchester and Salford at the Close of the XIX Century: Contemporary Biographies*, c. 1900).

(SIR) CHARLES THOMAS WHEELER (1892–1974) was responsible for the fountain sculpture, 'Sea Piece', in front of the art gallery, a gift of the Trustees of the Gallery in commemoration of the Gallery's Silver Jubilee and then centenary of the birth of Lady Lever (i.e., undertaken after Lever's own death). Wheeler was born in Wolverhampton and trained at the Royal Academy Schools. He was a favoured sculptor of Herbert Baker with whom he worked on the rebuilding of the Bank of England, being responsible for its bronze doors and frontage bas relief figures, with other work on South Africa House and the Jellicoe fountain in Trafalgar Square – this last perhaps the inspiration for the Trustees employing him. Additionally, he undertook a bust of the second Viscount in 1949 placed in the Lady Lever memorial loggia. He was president of the Royal Academy from 1956 to 1966.

Notes
1 Philip Ward Jackson, *Public Sculpture of The City of London*, 2003.
2 Terry Wyke and Harry Cocks, *Public Sculpture of Greater Manchester*, 2004.
3 Anthea Darlington and Neil Darlington, *St Pauls Church, Kersal Moor, Churchyard Trail*, 2011; W. Burnett Tracy and W. T. Pike, *Manchester and Salford at the Close of the XIX Century: Contemporary Biographies*, c. 1900.

List of Houses in the Village Proper

The following list is based on information from the former Village Estates Office and from the evidence of the original drawings now in the Unilever Archives collection. Dates refer to when each block was erected, which in some cases may differ from dates incorporated in decorative detailing. Original numbers of house units are shown in the second column.

Bath Street

1	1	Grayson & Ould	1896	
3–33	16	J. J. Talbot	1897	1896, date on building

Bebington Road

45–55	6	Grayson & Ould	1899	1897, date on building. Return of Boundary Road block
57–65	5	W. & S. Owen	1899	
67–79	7	E. Newton	1899	
81–87	4	T. M. Lockwood & Son	1899	
89–97	5	Wilson & Talbot	1899	
99–109	6	Douglas & Minshull	1906	1905, date on building

Bolton Road

1	2	W. Owen	1889	1889, date on building. Built as two houses
5–7	2	W. Owen	1889	
9–13	3	W. Owen	1889	
15	1	W. Owen	1889	
17–21	3	W. & S. Owen	1890	Converted to 9 apartments by Paddock Johnson Associates, 2006
61–69	5	W. Owen	1898	
71–75	3	Douglas & Minshull	1898	
2–12	6	W. Owen	1889	Converted to 3 houses
14–18	3	J. Lomax Simpson	1947?	Rebuilding of original block by W. Owen
20	1	Grayson & Ould	1896	Return of Cross Street block
22–42	12	W. Owen	1896	1895, date on building
60–62	2	J. Lomax Simpson	1914	Part of The Ginnel group
64–78	8	W. & S. Owen	1912	

Bridge Street

1–9	5	Douglas & Fordham	1894	1894, date on building
8–14	4	Grayson & Ould	1894	Rebuilt 1947
16–22	4	W. & S. Owen	1894	

Brook Street

3–4	2	Grayson & Ould	1906	
5–10	6	Grayson & Ould	1901	

Boundary Road

2–8	4	Grayson & Ould	1899	
10–16	4	Douglas & Fordham	1899	Rebuilt 1947
3–11	5	Grayson & Ould	1905	Built with 2 shops. Rebuilt 1947
13–33	11	Grayson & Ould	1905	Built with shop at No. 33
35–47	7	Grayson & Ould	1905	Built with shop at No. 35
Hesketh Hall	14	J. J. Talbot and Grayson & Ould	1903/ 1905	Converted to 14 apartments by Paddock Johnson Associates, 2014

The Causeway

1–4	4	Grayson & Ould	1901	
5–7	3	W. & S. Owen	1901	Return of Church Drive group
11		J. Lomax Simpson	1913	
8–12	5	J. Lomax Simpson	1913	1913, date on building
13–17	5	J. Lomax Simpson	1913	Block including 47–50 Queen Mary's Drive, remodelled as flats
18–22	5	Wilson & Talbot	1901	

Central Road

1	1	Deacon & Horsburgh	1907	
3–13	6	W. N. Adams	1907	
15–27	7	Garnet, Wright and Garnet and F. J. Barnish	1907	
Osborne Court: Nos. 1–2 and Newton Lodge		Paddock Johnson Associates	1999	Sheltered housing scheme
Osborne Court: Nos. 3–6		Paddock Johnson Associates	1999	
Osborne Court: Nos. 7–10		Paddock Johnson Associates	1999	
Manor Lodge		J. Lomax Simpson	1939– 40	Former Nurses' Home, converted to flats, c. 2004, Paddock Johnson Associates
2–14	7	Bradshaw, Gass and Hope	1906	Block including 11–21 Primrose Hill, remodelled as flats
16–24	5	F. J. Barnish	1911	
26–34	5	F. J. Barnish	1911	
36–44	5	H. Bloomfield Bare	1906	
46–64	10	J. Lomax Simpson	1906	
66–70	3	J. Lomax Simpson	1906	Return of Lower Road block

Church Drive

1–5	5	W. & S. Owen	1901	
6–13	8	Grayson & Ould	1905	
14–16	3	Not identified	1902	Part of Nos. 25–27 Windy Bank

Circular Drive

2–16	8	W. & S. Owen	1899	
18–26	5	Grayson & Ould	1906	
28–38	6	W. & S. Owen	1899	

Corniche Road

1–5	5	W. Owen	1898	Return of New Chester Road group
7–15	5	Douglas & Fordham	1898	1897, date on building
17–23	4	E. L. Lutyens	1899	
25–29	3	Wilson & Talbot	1899	
31–35	3	Jonathan Simpson	1899	1897, date on building
37–41	3	Wilson & Talbot	1898	
43–47	3	T. T. Rees	1898	1897, date on building
49–53	3	E. Kirby	1899	
55–59	3	Grayson & Ould	1898	
61–67	4	H. A. Matear	1898	
69	1	W. Owen	1898	Return of Bolton Road group

Cross Street

1–9	5	Grayson & Ould	1896

The Ginnel

1–5	3	J. Lomax Simpson	1914
7–23	9	J. Lomax Simpson	1914
25–35	6	J. Lomax Simpson	1914

Greendale Road

Duke of York's Cottages	18	J. Lomax Simpson	1934	Pensioners' cottages, 1933, date on building
3–6	4	J. Lomax Simpson	1925	
6A–6H	8	J. Lomax Simpson	1926	
6K–7–10	5	Grayson & Ould	1901	Rebuilt J. Lomax Simpson, 1926, for formation of new axial approach to Gallery
11–17	7	J. J. Talbot	1902	
18–24	7	Grayson & Ould	1899	
25–29	5	Ernest George & Yeates	1901	
30–32	3	Grayson & Ould	1901	
33–39	7	Ernest George & Yeates	1901	
40–43	3	Grayson & Ould	1901	
44–48	5	Wilson & Talbot	1901	
49–53	5	Grayson & Ould	1901	
54–58	5	Pain and Blease	1901	
59–63	5	M. B. Adams	1899	
64–70	7	Wilson & Talbot	1899	
71–74	4	W. Owen	1891	
75–78	4	W. Owen	1891	
79–82	4	W. Owen	1891	
83–88	6	Grayson & Ould	1891	Includes the village's first shop, later Post Office, now Tea Room
89–92	4	W. Owen	1894	
(93–96)	-	(Maxwell and Tuke)	(1896)	(Former Girls' Dormitory)
97–100	4	Grayson & Ould	1894	

Jubilee Crescent

1–15	15	J. Lomax Simpson	1938

King George's Drive

1–3	2	J. Lomax Simpson	1913	
5–20	18	J. Lomax Simpson	1913	
21–22	2	J. Lomax Simpson	1913	Part of Girls' Club group
(23)		(J. Lomax Simpson)	(1913)	(Former Girls' Club, now Museum)

Lodge Lane

2–10	5	W. & S. Owen	1900	
12–20	5	Grayson & Ould	1899	Block including 69–75 Pool Bank, remodelled as flats

Lower Road

1–7	4	Grayson & Ould	1901	Return of Primrose Hill block
9–13	6	Wilson & Talbot	1901	
15–27	7	C. Reilly	1906	
29–33	3	J. Lomax Simpson	1907	
35–49	8	J. Lomax Simpson	1906	
51–59	5	J. Lomax Simpson	1906	Return of Central Road block

New Chester Road

128–132	3	Douglas & Minshull	1899	Return of Boundary Road block
134–146	7	Wilson & Talbot	1900	
148–156	5	H. A. Matear	1899	
158–168	6	H. Beswick	1899	
170–176	4	W. Owen	1900	
178–190	7	Ernest George & Yeates	1899	1897, date on building
192–198	4	Grayson & Ould	1899	
200–210	6	H. A. Matear	1899	
212–216	3	W. & S. Owen	1899	
218–222	3	W. & S. Owen	1899	
224–228	3	Grayson & Ould	1898	
230–232	2	Grayson & Ould	1898	
234–238	3	Grayson & Ould	1898	
240–242	2	Grayson & Ould	1898	
244–248	3	Douglas & Fordham	1898	
250–254	3	W. Owen	1898	1896, date on building
256–260	3	W. Owen	1898	
262–266	3	W. Owen	1898	1896, date on building
268–274	4	Douglas & Minshull	1898	
276–282	4	W. & S. Owen	1898	1896, date on building
284–286	2	Douglas & Fordham	1898	
288–292	3	Grayson & Ould	1898	
294–296	2	Douglas & Fordham	1898	
298–300	2	J. Simpson	1898	
302–304	2	Grayson & Ould	1898	
306–308	2	T. T. Rees	1898	
310–312	2	Grayson & Ould	1898	
314–318	3	Grayson & Ould	1898	
320–322	2	Grayson & Ould	1898	
324–326	2	Grayson & Ould	1898	

Park Road

1–7	4	W. Owen	1892	1892, date on building
9–17	5	W. Owen	1892	
19–23	3	Douglas & Fordham	1892	Includes Bridge Cottage,
2–4	2	W. Owen	1892	1892, date on building
6–12	4	W. Owen	1894	
14–22	5	W. Owen	1893	1893, date on building
24	1	W. Owen	1894	Return of Bridge Street block
26	1	Douglas & Fordham	1893	Return of Bridge Street block
28–36	5	W. Owen	1893	1893, date on building
38–48	6	T. M. Lockwood	1895	
50–52	2	Grayson & Ould	1894	Return of Poets' Corner block

Poets' Corner

2–8	4	Grayson & Ould	1894	

Pool Bank

1–7	4	W. & S. Owen	1899	
9–17	5	Wilson & Talbot	1902	
19–25	4	H. A. Matear	1899	No. 19, rebuilt 1947
27–39	7	Wilson & Talbot	1901	31–35, rebuilt 1947
41–53	7	Grayson & Ould	1899	1898, date on building
55–67	7	Douglas & Minshull	1899	
69–75	4	Grayson & Ould	1899	Block including 12–20 Lodge Lane, remodelled as flats
2–6	3	Grayson & Ould	1906	
8–14	4	Grayson & Ould	1907	
16–22	4	Grayson & Ould	1907	
24–34	6	Grayson & Ould	1907	
Osborne Court Nos. 16–20		Paddock Johnson Associates	1999	
Osborne Court Nos. 11–15		Paddock Johnson Associates	1999	
Philip Leverhulme Lodge	10	Paddock Johnson Associates	2000	

Primrose Hill

1–9	5	Deacon & Horsburgh	1907	
11–21	6	Bradshaw & Gass	1906	Block including 2–14 Central Road, remodelled as flats
23–35	7	Ormrod and Pomeroy	1906	
37–45	5	Grayson & Ould	1901	Return of Lower Road block
47–53	4	J. Lomax Simpson	1925	
55–57	2	J. Lomax Simpson	1925	
2–4	2	W. & S. Owen	1899	
6–14	5	Douglas & Minshull	1899	
16–28	7	H. A. Matear	1899	
30–38	5	J. Simpson	1899	
40–50	6	E. Kirby	1899	
52–56	3	M. B. Adams	1899	

Queen Mary's Drive

10–14	5	J. Lomax Simpson	1925	
15–22	8	J. Lomax Simpson	1926	Return of 5 Windy Bank
23–30	8	J. Lomax Simpson	1913	
31–46	16	J. Lomax Simpson	1913	
47–50	4	J. Lomax Simpson	1913	Block including 13–17 The Causeway, remodelled as flats

Riverside

1–8	8	Grayson & Ould	1895	
9–10	2	J. J. Talbot	1897	Return of Bath Street group

Underley Terrace

7–9	2	Grayson & Ould	1905	

Water Street

1–7	4	W. & S. Owen	1912	
9–21	7	W. & S. Owen	1912	
2–4	2	J. Lomax Simpson	1914	Return of The Ginnel group
1 – 21 Woodhead Row	21	Paddock Johnson Associates	2009	21 apartments

Wharf Street

Darcy Court		Paddock Johnson Associates	2015	58 sheltered housing apartments

Windy Bank

1–3	2	J. Lomax Simpson	1926	
5	1	J. Lomax Simpson	1926	Return of Queen Mary's Drive block
2–4	2	J. Lomax Simpson	1926	Rebuild of earlier Grayson & Ould block
6–11	6	Grayson & Ould	1902	Part of block truncated in 1926
12–18	7	Grayson & Ould	1902	
19–22	4	J. Lomax Simpson	1913	Part of Girls' Club group
23–24	2	Grayson & Ould	1907	
25–27	3	Not identified	1902	1900, date on building. Part of Nos. 14–16 Church Drive

Wood Street

1–7	4	W. Owen	1894	
9–15	4	H. A. Matear	1894	1892, date on building
17–23	4	Douglas & Fordham	1894	1892, date on building
25	1	W. Owen	1894	Return of Bridge Street block
27–35	5	Grayson & Ould	1895	
37–47	6	Grayson & Ould	1895	
49–55	4	Douglas & Fordham	1895	

Select Bibliography

Armstrong, Barry and Wendy Armstrong, *The Arts and Crafts Movement in the North West of England: A Handbook*, 2005.

Beeson, E. W., *Port Sunlight: The Model Village of England*, 1911.

Boumphrey, Ian and Gavin Hunter, *Yesterday's Wirral: Port Sunlight. A Pictorial History, 1888 to 1953*, 2002.

Creese, Walter L., *The Search for Environment*, 1966.

Darbyshire, Alfred, *The Book of Olde Manchester and Salford, Royal Jubilee Exhibition*, 1887.

Davison, T. Raffles, *Port Sunlight*, 1916.

Edwards, E. H., *Messrs. Lever's New Soap Works, Port Sunlight, Cheshire. Full Reports of the Cutting the First Sod and Proceedings at the Inaugural Banquet*, 1888.

George, W. L., *Labour and Housing at Port Sunlight*, 1909.

Hartwell, Clare, Matthew Hyde, Edward Hubbard and Nikolaus Pevsner, *The Buildings of England: Cheshire*, 2nd edn, 2011.

Hubbard, Edward, *The Work of John Douglas*, ed. Peter Howell. Published by the Victorian Society, 1991.

Hubbard, Edward and Michael Shippobottom, 'Architecture', in *Lord Leverhulme: Catalogue of an Exhibition Presented at the Royal Academy of Arts by Unilever, to Mark their Golden Jubilee*, 1980. Details given of sources include references to many of the numerous features relating to Port Sunlight which appeared in the professional and technical press; also cited are many items in the indispensable archive held by the Unilever Archives at Port Sunlight.

Hunter, Gavin, *100 Years of Innovation: The History of Unilever Research Port Sunlight*, 2000.

——— *The Life of Lady Lever*, 2013.

Jolly, W. P., *Lord Leverhulme*, 1976.

Knox, Andrew, *Coming Clean*, 1976.

Lever, W. H. (later Viscount Leverhulme), *The Buildings Erected at Port Sunlight and Thornton Hough*, 1902; 2nd edn, 1905.

Second Viscount Leverhulme, *Viscount Leverhulme by his Son*, 1927.

Lewis, Brian, *So Clean: Lord Leverhulme, Soap and Civilization*, 2008.

Lister, Mike, *The Industrial Railways of Port Sunlight and Bromborough Port*, 2nd edn, 1988.

Macqueen, Adam, *The King of Sunlight: How William Lever Cleaned up the World*, 2004.

Mawson, Thomas H., *Civic Art*, 1911.

Miller, Mervyn, *English Garden Cities: An Introduction*, 2010.

Morris, Edward and Emma Roberts, *Public Sculpture of Britain: Public Sculpture of Cheshire and Merseyside (excluding Liverpool)*, 2012.

Port Sunlight Village Trust, *Conservation Management Plan*, 2018.

Seaborne, Malcolm and Roy Lowe, *The English School: Its Architecture and Organisation*, vol. 2, *1870–1970*, 1977.

Shippobottom, Michael, 'The Building of the Lady Lever Art Gallery', in Edward Morris (ed.), *Art and Business in Edwardian England: The Making of the Lady Lever Art Gallery*, 1992.

—— 'Port Sunlight: Continuity and Change', in Peter Burman (ed.), *The Conservation of Twentieth-Century Buildings*, proceedings of a conference at the Institute of Advanced Architectural Studies, University of York, 1993.

—— 'C. H. Reilly and the First Lord Leverhulme', in Joseph Sharples, Alan Powers and Michael Shippobottom, *Charles Reilly and the Liverpool School of Architecture, 1904–1933: Catalogue of an Exhibition at the Walker Art Gallery, Liverpool*, 25 October 1996–2 February 1997.

—— 'Unmatched for Drama: Lord Leverhulme's Rivington Estate', *Country Life*, 13 September 1984.

Williams, Edmund, *The First Hundred Years: 1888–1988. The Short History of a Famous Factory*, 1988.

Wilson, Charles, *The History of Unilever*, 1954.